Disclaimer: Anecdotes, Case Studies, and Examples

Throughout this book, you will come across various anecdotes, case studies, and examples that are used to illustrate and emphasize the strategies and concepts discussed. It is important to note that these anecdotes are not based on real individuals or specific events. They are created for illustrative purposes only, aiming to better convey the underlying principles and ideas.

While the stories and examples shared are not rooted in real-life experiences, the strategies, techniques, and recommendations presented are based on proven industry practices and research. They are designed to provide practical, actionable advice that you can apply to your HVAC business.

WRENCHES TO RICHES

The Ultimate Guide to Building a Thriving HVAC Business

Epic Network

CONTENTS

INTRODUCTION

Welcome to "From Wrenches to Riches: The Ultimate Guide to Building a Thriving HVAC Business"! If you are an HVAC professional with aspirations of taking your business to new heights, then you have come to the right place. This book is your comprehensive roadmap to success, filled with practical advice, actionable strategies, and real-life examples that will help you build a thriving HVAC business and achieve your entrepreneurial dreams.

Imagine transforming your passion for heating, ventilation, and air conditioning into a profitable and fulfilling venture. Whether you are just starting out or looking to scale your existing HVAC business, this book is designed to provide you with the knowledge, tools, and inspiration you need to make it happen. We will delve into various areas of expertise, including business development, marketing, sales, customer service, leadership, and more, to equip you with a holistic understanding of what it takes to thrive in the HVAC industry.

To make this journey engaging and relatable, we will embark on this adventure alongside several HVAC professionals who have turned their businesses into tremendous success stories. Their experiences, stories, and insights will serve as guiding beacons throughout the book, illustrating the real-world challenges and triumphs that you may encounter along the way.

Statistics reveal the immense potential and opportunities within the HVAC industry. According to a report by Research and Markets, the global HVAC market is expected to reach a value of $251.6 billion by 2027. This growth is driven by factors such as increasing energy efficiency requirements, rising demand for advanced HVAC technologies, and the need for sustainable solutions.

However, success in the HVAC industry is not solely determined by technical expertise. It requires a blend of business acumen, marketing prowess, exceptional customer service, and effective leadership. This book will guide you through each of these critical areas, providing you with actionable advice and proven strategies to help you stand out from the crowd.

Throughout the chapters, we will encounter professionals like Mark, a passionate HVAC technician who transformed his small local business into a regional leader by embracing innovation and building a stellar team. We will also meet Sarah, who successfully transitioned from technician to a confident leader, balancing technical skills with managerial expertise. Their stories, along with many others, will inspire and provide valuable insights that you can apply to your own HVAC business journey.

In addition to these captivating stories, we will dive into practical topics such as developing an entrepreneurial mindset, crafting a solid business plan, creating a compelling brand identity, designing effective marketing strategies, determining optimal pricing strategies, and mastering the art of consultative selling. We will explore the nuances of delivering exceptional customer service, scaling up your business for long-term success, and developing your leadership skills.

To make this guide even more actionable, we have included resources, templates, and checklists in the appendix section.

These tools will serve as invaluable companions as you implement the strategies and recommendations outlined throughout the book.

So, whether you are an HVAC technician dreaming of starting your own business, a small business owner seeking growth and expansion, or a seasoned entrepreneur looking to refine your strategies, "From Wrenches to Riches" is your go-to resource. It is time to unlock the full potential of your HVAC business and embark on a journey of growth, profitability, and personal fulfillment.

Buckle up and get ready to navigate the exciting world of HVAC business mastery. With each turn of the page, you will gain practical insights, inspiration, and actionable strategies that will empower you to transform your HVAC business from wrenches to riches. Let's embark on this adventure together and build the thriving HVAC business you've always dreamed of!

CHAPTER 1

Passion to Profit: The Entrepreneurial Mindset in the HVAC Industry

Imagine waking up every day excited to go to work, knowing that you're not only doing what you love but also building a successful business. That's the power of combining passion with a strong entrepreneurial mindset. In this chapter, we'll explore how to harness your passion for the HVAC industry and cultivate the mindset necessary to turn it into a profitable venture. We'll dive into stories, examples, and strategies that will empower you to overcome challenges, embrace opportunities, and pave the way for your success in the HVAC business.

Unleashing Your Passion

Passion is the driving force behind any successful venture. It fuels motivation, creativity, and perseverance, making it an essential ingredient in building a thriving HVAC business. Consider the story of Joe, a young technician who started his HVAC business out of pure love for the trade. Joe's passion was evident in every project he undertook. His attention to detail and dedication to customer satisfaction set him apart from the competition. It wasn't long before word spread about Joe's exceptional work, and his business began to flourish.

Passion goes beyond technical skills; it encompasses a genuine desire to make a difference in people's lives through HVAC services. It's about understanding that you're not just fixing machines, but improving the comfort and well-being of your customers. When you approach your work with passion, it shines through in the quality of your service, building trust and loyalty among your clientele.

Cultivating an Entrepreneurial Mindset:

Having a passion for HVAC is a great start, but to build a thriving business, you also need an entrepreneurial mindset. This mindset involves thinking like a business owner, seizing opportunities, and embracing a growth-oriented approach.

Embracing a Growth Mindset

A growth mindset is the belief that your abilities and intelligence can be developed through dedication and hard work. This mindset is essential because it enables you to embrace challenges and view failures as opportunities for learning and improvement.

If you face a major setback when a client is dissatisfied with their service. Instead of feeling defeated, see it as an opportunity to assess the process and make improvements. Seek out feedback from the client, implement changes, and turn the negative experience into a positive one.

By adopting a growth mindset, you can continue to learn and refine your skills, ultimately leading to the growth and success of your HVAC business.

Embracing Risk-Taking

Entrepreneurship inherently involves taking risks. It's about stepping out of your comfort zone and seizing opportunities, even when they come with uncertainty. Successful entrepreneurs understand that calculated risks are essential for growth and innovation.

Mark, a seasoned HVAC technician who decided to start

his own business. Initially, he was hesitant about leaving the security of his steady job, but he knew that to fulfill his entrepreneurial dreams, he had to take the leap. Mark researched the market, analyzed the competition, and created a comprehensive business plan. Despite the risks, Mark's venture paid off. His willingness to embrace calculated risks and pursue his passion led to the establishment of a highly successful HVAC business.

Building a Network of Support

Building a thriving HVAC business requires a network of support. Surrounding yourself with like-minded individuals, mentors, and industry experts can provide valuable guidance, insights, and support during your entrepreneurial journey.

Here's Alex, a young entrepreneur who recognized the importance of building relationships within the HVAC industry. Alex actively sought out networking events, joined professional associations, and connected with experienced professionals. Through these connections, he gained valuable advice, access to new opportunities, and even potential partnerships.

The power of a strong network can't be overstated; it can open doors, provide support, and even lead to collaborative ventures that drive your HVAC business forward.

Overcoming Challenges

Building a thriving HVAC business isn't without its challenges. However, with the right mindset, you can turn these obstacles into stepping stones for success. Let's explore a few common challenges and strategies for overcoming them.

Competition

The HVAC industry is highly competitive, with numerous businesses vying for customers. To stand out, you need to differentiate yourself from the competition. One effective strategy is to focus on your unique selling proposition (USP). Identify what sets your business apart and emphasize it in your marketing efforts. For example, if you specialize in energy-efficient solutions, highlight your expertise in that area and the benefits it brings to customers.

Additionally, consider the power of exceptional customer service. Going above and beyond for your clients creates loyal customers who will not only return but also recommend your services to others. Treat every customer interaction as an opportunity to exceed expectations and leave a lasting positive impression.

Skilled Labor Shortage

The HVAC industry is facing a shortage of skilled technicians, making it challenging to find and retain qualified professionals. To overcome this hurdle, consider investing in employee training and development programs. By offering ongoing education and opportunities for growth, you can attract and retain top talent.

Another approach is to build strong relationships with technical schools and trade programs. Actively participate in job fairs, offer internships or apprenticeships, and provide mentorship opportunities. By engaging with emerging talent, you can bridge the skills gap and cultivate a pipeline of skilled technicians for your business.

Adapting to Technological Advancements

The HVAC industry is evolving rapidly, with advancements in technology transforming the way services are delivered. Embracing these technological advancements is key to staying competitive and improving operational efficiency. For example, smart thermostats, remote diagnostics, and energy management systems can enhance customer experiences and streamline operations.

Educate yourself and your team about emerging technologies, attend industry conferences, and explore partnerships with technology providers. By incorporating these innovations into your business, you can enhance your service offerings and provide a seamless customer experience.

Seasonal Demand Fluctuations

HVAC businesses often experience seasonal peaks and valleys in demand. To navigate these fluctuations, it's crucial to have a well-thought-out resource management strategy. During busy seasons, ensure you have enough staff and equipment to handle the increased workload. During slower periods, focus on proactive marketing and sales efforts to generate leads and maintain a steady stream of business.

Consider offering maintenance contracts or service packages to incentivize customers to schedule regular check-ups, even during non-peak seasons. These contracts not only provide recurring revenue but also help maintain a consistent workload throughout the year.

In the HVAC industry, passion and an entrepreneurial mindset are essential ingredients for building a thriving business. By combining your love for the trade with the mindset of an entrepreneur, you can overcome challenges, seize opportunities, and create a successful HVAC venture.

Remember, success is not guaranteed overnight. It requires dedication, continuous learning, and the willingness to adapt to changes in the industry. By embracing a growth mindset, taking calculated risks, building a network of support, and finding innovative ways to differentiate yourself, you can turn your passion for HVAC into a profitable and fulfilling business.

We will delve into the practical strategies, tips, and actionable advice that will guide you through the various aspects of running a successful HVAC business. From branding and marketing to pricing strategies, customer service excellence to scaling up operations, our goal is to equip you with the knowledge and tools you need to thrive in the HVAC industry. So, let's dive in and embark on this exciting journey together!

Before you move on to the next section:

1. Reflect on your passion for the HVAC industry and identify specific aspects that fuel your drive. Write down three actionable steps you can take to further explore and nurture your passion within the entrepreneurial context.

2. Develop an entrepreneurial mindset by seeking out learning opportunities. Identify one workshop, seminar, or online course related to entrepreneurship or business management that you can attend or enroll in within the next three months.

3. Create a list of potential challenges and opportunities you may encounter as an HVAC entrepreneur. Brainstorm strategies or solutions for each item on the list and commit to implementing at least one of these strategies in the next month.

CHAPTER 2

*Crafting Your Business Blueprint:
From Vision to Reality*

Now that you've cultivated your passion for the HVAC industry and embraced an entrepreneurial mindset, it's time to turn your vision into a concrete business plan. Now, we'll guide you through the process of defining your business vision and goals.

We'll explore how a clear vision serves as your North Star, guiding your decisions and actions. Additionally, we'll delve into setting specific, measurable, achievable, relevant, and time-bound (SMART) goals to drive your HVAC business forward.

The Power of a Clear Vision

A clear vision acts as a guiding light for your HVAC business. It's a vivid picture of what you want to achieve, the impact you want to make, and the legacy you want to leave behind. Your vision serves as the foundation upon which your business is built.

Meet Laura, a successful HVAC business owner. Her vision was to become the go-to provider of energy-efficient HVAC solutions in her region. This vision guided her decision-making process, from investing in training her technicians on the latest energy-efficient technologies to implementing sustainable practices within her business operations. By staying true to her vision, Laura was able to carve out a niche for her business and build a strong reputation as an industry leader.

Defining Your Vision

To define your business vision, start by asking yourself meaningful questions. What impact do you want to make in the HVAC industry? How do you want your customers to perceive your business? What values do you want to embody? Consider both short-term and long-term aspirations.

Next, distill your answers into a clear and concise statement. Your vision statement should inspire and motivate you and your team. It should be a reflection of your passion, values, and long-term goals.

For example, your vision statement might be: "To be the premier provider of top-quality HVAC services, recognized for our exceptional customer experiences, innovation, and commitment to sustainability."

Setting SMART Goals

With a clear vision in place, it's time to set SMART goals that will drive your HVAC business forward. SMART goals are specific, measurable, achievable, relevant, and time-bound. Let's break down each component:

Specific: Your goals should be clear and well-defined. Avoid vague or generic statements. Instead, be precise about what you want to accomplish. For example, instead of saying, "Increase revenue," specify, "Increase revenue by 15% within the next fiscal year."

Measurable: Your goals should be quantifiable so that you can track progress and success. Define metrics or key performance indicators (KPIs) that will help you gauge your progress. For instance, you might track the number of new service contracts secured per month or customer satisfaction ratings.

<u>Achievable:</u> While it's important to set ambitious goals, ensure they are realistic and attainable. Consider your available resources, capabilities, and market conditions. Setting unrealistic goals can lead to frustration and discouragement.

<u>Relevant:</u> Align your goals with your business vision and priorities. Ensure they are relevant to your long-term objectives. If your vision is centered around energy efficiency, a relevant goal might be to become certified in energy-efficient HVAC systems.

<u>Time-bound:</u> Set a clear timeline for achieving your goals. Establish deadlines and milestones to keep you accountable and motivated. This time-bound aspect adds a sense of urgency and helps you stay on track.

By setting SMART goals, you create a roadmap for success. Each goal becomes a stepping stone toward realizing your vision and propelling your HVAC business forward.

Defining Your Business Vision

Defining your business vision and setting SMART goals are essential steps in building a thriving HVAC business. Your vision acts as a guiding force, directing your decisions and actions.

With a clear vision, you have a destination in mind, and setting SMART goals provides the roadmap to reach that destination. By making your goals specific, measurable, achievable, relevant, and time-bound, you ensure that they are tangible and actionable.

Think of your vision and goals as the compass and the milestones on your entrepreneurial journey. They keep you focused, motivated, and aligned with your long-term aspirations. As you progress, you can celebrate each milestone achieved, knowing that you're one step closer to turning your HVAC business dreams into reality.

To keep your vision and goals alive, share them with your team. Engage your employees in the process, empowering them to contribute their ideas and perspectives. When everyone understands and aligns with the vision, it creates a shared sense of purpose and commitment. Together, you can work towards achieving those goals, supporting one another along the way.

Remember, your vision and goals are not set in stone. As your business evolves and the industry changes, it's important to review and adapt them accordingly. Regularly assess your progress, celebrate successes, and learn from any setbacks. Adjustments may be necessary, whether it's refining your vision to align with market trends or revising your goals to reflect new opportunities.

So, let's keep that passion burning, embrace an entrepreneurial mindset, define a clear vision, and set SMART goals that will propel your HVAC business to new heights. Your journey towards building a thriving HVAC business starts here, and we're excited to accompany you every step of the way.

How to Develop a Growth Mindset: Unlocking Your Potential for Success

A growth mindset is a powerful mindset that can propel you towards success in all aspects of life, including your HVAC business. It is the belief that your abilities and intelligence can be developed through dedication and hard work. With a growth mindset, you embrace challenges, learn from failures, and continuously seek opportunities for growth and improvement. Here, we will explore the seven step-by-step instructions on how to develop a growth mindset and unlock your potential for success.

Step 1: Embrace the Power of Yet

The first step in developing a growth mindset is to embrace the power of the word "yet." Whenever you encounter a challenge or feel like you're not good at something, remind yourself that you just haven't mastered it yet. The word "yet" signifies that you are on a journey of growth and learning. For example, if you think, "I'm not good at sales," reframe it as, "I'm not good at sales yet, but with practice and learning, I can improve."

Step 2: Embrace Challenges and View Failure as a Learning Opportunity

Embracing challenges is a fundamental aspect of developing a growth mindset. Instead of shying away from difficulties, actively seek out opportunities that stretch your abilities. Recognize that challenges are chances for growth and development. When faced with setbacks or failures, view them as learning opportunities rather than reasons to give up. Ask yourself, "What can I learn from this? How can I improve?" This mindset shift will help you approach challenges with resilience and a desire to learn.

Step 3: Cultivate a Love for Learning

To develop a growth mindset, cultivate a love for learning. Embrace a mindset of curiosity and a thirst for knowledge. Seek out new information, skills, and perspectives. Expand your industry knowledge by reading books, attending seminars, or taking online courses related to the HVAC field. Actively engage in professional development opportunities and encourage your team members to do the same. Remember, the more you learn, the more you grow.

Step 4: Reframe Criticism and Feedback

Reframing criticism and feedback is crucial in developing a growth mindset. Instead of taking feedback personally or seeing it as an attack on your abilities, view it as valuable input for improvement. Embrace constructive criticism as an opportunity to learn and grow. Actively seek feedback from your team, customers, and mentors, and use it to refine your skills and approaches. Remember, feedback is not a reflection of your worth as a person but an opportunity to become better.

Step 5: Surround Yourself with Growth-Oriented People

The people you surround yourself with can significantly influence your mindset. Surround yourself with growth-oriented individuals who inspire and motivate you. Seek out mentors who have achieved success in the HVAC industry and learn from their experiences. Engage with like-minded professionals through networking events, industry associations, or online communities. By surrounding yourself with growth-oriented people, you create an environment that supports and encourages your mindset development.

Step 6: Embrace Effort and Persistence

Effort and persistence are key ingredients in developing a growth mindset. Recognize that success is not solely determined by natural talent or intelligence but by consistent effort and dedication. Embrace the value of hard work and persevere even when faced with obstacles. Celebrate the small victories along the way and use them as fuel to keep going. Remember, it's the combination of effort, resilience, and continuous learning that leads to long-term success.

Step 7: Celebrate Growth and Progress

Finally, celebrate your growth and progress along the way. Acknowledge and appreciate the steps you've taken and the improvements you've made. Reflect on your achievements, whether big or small, and use them as reminders of your journey towards developing a growth mindset. Celebrate not only the end results but also the effort, resilience, and learning that went into your progress. By acknowledging your growth, you reinforce the belief that you are capable of continuous improvement and success.

Developing a growth mindset is a transformative journey that can unlock your potential for success in your HVAC business and beyond. By embracing the power of "yet," viewing challenges as opportunities, and reframing feedback, you can cultivate a mindset that embraces growth, learning, and resilience. Surround yourself with growth-oriented individuals, celebrate your progress, and embrace the value of effort and persistence. Remember, developing a growth mindset is not an overnight process—it requires consistent practice and self-reflection.

As you continue to develop a growth mindset, you'll find that you approach challenges with a sense of optimism and a desire to learn. You'll view failures as stepping stones to success and setbacks as opportunities for growth. With a growth mindset, you'll continuously seek opportunities to expand your skills, improve your business strategies, and adapt to the ever-evolving HVAC industry.

So, start your journey today. Embrace challenges, love learning, seek feedback, and celebrate your growth. By cultivating a growth mindset, you'll unlock your true potential and pave the way for success in your HVAC business and all areas of your life.

Embracing Risk-Taking: Igniting Growth and Innovation in Your HVAC Business

Embracing risk-taking is a fundamental aspect of building a thriving HVAC business. While the idea of taking risks may seem daunting, it is through calculated risk-taking that entrepreneurs propel their businesses forward, ignite growth, and foster innovation. In this chapter, we will explore the importance of embracing risk-taking and provide real-life examples, case studies, and statistics to illustrate its impact on HVAC businesses. By understanding the benefits and strategies for effective risk-taking, you can harness its power to drive your business towards success.

The Benefits of Risk-Taking

1. Stimulating Innovation:

Taking risks encourages innovation within your HVAC business. When you step outside your comfort zone, you open the door to new ideas, approaches, and solutions. Innovation often arises from pushing boundaries and challenging the status quo. Consider the case of ABC HVAC, a company that took the risk of incorporating cutting-edge energy-efficient technologies into their services. This move not only differentiated them from competitors but also positioned them as industry leaders, attracting customers who valued sustainability and cost savings.

2. Seizing Opportunities:

By embracing risk-taking, you position yourself to seize opportunities that others may overlook. Opportunities often come disguised as risks, and it is those who are willing to take calculated leaps that reap the rewards. For instance, XYZ HVAC recognized the growing demand for smart home automation systems. They took the risk of investing in the necessary training and equipment to offer these services. As a result, they secured contracts with tech-savvy homeowners, expanded their customer base, and boosted their revenue significantly.

3. Overcoming Stagnation:

Taking calculated risks helps you overcome stagnation and complacency. In a rapidly evolving HVAC industry, staying stagnant can hinder your growth and jeopardize your competitive edge. By embracing risk-taking, you challenge yourself to evolve, adapt, and explore new possibilities.

Joe's Heating & Cooling, a long-established HVAC business that faced declining market share. Recognizing the need for change, they took the risk of rebranding, revamping their marketing strategies, and targeting a younger demographic.

This bold move breathed new life into their business, attracting a fresh wave of customers and rejuvenating their revenue streams.

Strategies for Effective Risk-Taking

Research and Analysis

Before taking risks, thorough research and analysis are crucial. Gather relevant data, industry insights, and market trends to inform your decisions. For instance, analyze customer demands, competitive landscapes, and emerging technologies to identify potential risks worth pursuing. By conducting due diligence, you minimize blind leaps and make informed decisions.

Calculated Risks

While risk-taking involves stepping into the unknown, it is essential to take calculated risks rather than reckless ones. Evaluate the potential rewards against the potential consequences. Assess the probability of success, potential impact on your business, and your capacity to mitigate potential downsides. By taking calculated risks, you balance innovation and growth with prudent decision-making.

Test and Iterate

In some cases, taking smaller, incremental risks and testing the waters can be beneficial. Consider implementing pilot programs or conducting small-scale experiments to validate assumptions and gather feedback. This iterative approach allows you to learn from early successes and failures, refine your strategies, and adjust your course as necessary. The HVAC company DEF Services, for example, wanted to expand their services into a new geographical area. Instead of diving headfirst, they launched a pilot program in a select neighborhood to gauge customer response and fine-tune their operations before scaling up.

Build a Support Network

Surround yourself with a network of mentors, industry peers, and advisors who can provide guidance and support as you navigate risks. Connect with organizations and associations that foster a culture of risk-taking and innovation. Engaging with like-minded professionals can provide valuable insights, fresh perspectives, and a support system that encourages you to embrace risk-taking. The experiences and advice shared by others in the industry can help you make more informed decisions and navigate potential challenges.

Let's delve into examples of HVAC businesses that have successfully embraced risk-taking and reaped the rewards:

CoolTech Solutions:

Recognizing the growing demand for renewable energy solutions, CoolTech Solutions took a calculated risk by expanding their services to include solar panel installations. By doing so, they tapped into a rapidly expanding market, attracted environmentally conscious customers, and positioned themselves as a comprehensive energy solutions provider. This strategic risk paid off with a significant increase in revenue and a competitive advantage over other HVAC companies.

AirComfort Systems:

Seeking to differentiate themselves in a saturated market,

AirComfort Systems decided to invest in customer experience. They took the risk of implementing a 24/7 customer support line, ensuring prompt responses to inquiries and service requests. This commitment to customer service led to a surge in positive reviews, customer referrals, and increased customer loyalty. The risk they took in prioritizing customer experience paid off in long-term business growth.

EcoAir Heating & Cooling:

In response to the rising demand for eco-friendly HVAC solutions, EcoAir Heating & Cooling ventured into geothermal heating and cooling systems. This was a significant risk, as the technology was relatively new and required specialized knowledge. However, by investing in training, collaborating with industry experts, and marketing themselves as geothermal specialists, they positioned themselves as pioneers in the field. This risk not only attracted a niche market of environmentally conscious customers but also opened doors to government contracts and industry recognition.

Embracing Risk Taking

Embracing risk-taking is not only crucial but necessary for the growth and success of HVAC businesses. By stimulating innovation, seizing opportunities, and overcoming stagnation, calculated risk-taking sets the stage for business growth, differentiation, and competitive advantage. Remember to conduct thorough research, take calculated risks, test and iterate, and build a support network. Real-life examples and statistics further highlight the impact of risk-taking in the HVAC industry.

As you navigate the HVAC business landscape, be open to

stepping outside your comfort zone, challenging conventions, and exploring new possibilities. Embrace the calculated risks that align with your business goals and industry trends. By doing so, you position your HVAC business for sustained growth, innovation, and long-term success. So, dare to take risks, and let your HVAC business soar to new heights!

Building a Network for Success in Your HVAC Business

Building a strong support network is essential for the success of your HVAC business. Engaging with mentors, industry peers, and experts provides valuable insights, support, and resources that can propel your business forward. In this chapter, we will explore step-by-step processes for effectively engaging for support and illustrate each point with case studies, examples, interviews, and research. By cultivating meaningful connections and leveraging the expertise of others, you can navigate challenges, gain new perspectives, and unlock opportunities for growth.

Step 1: Identifying Key Support Networks:

The first step in engaging for support is identifying the key networks and communities relevant to the HVAC industry. These networks can include industry associations, professional organizations, online forums, trade shows, and local business groups. Research and identify the networks that align with your business goals, values, and target audience.

Johnson HVAC Services, a growing HVAC business, recognized the importance of engaging with industry networks to foster their success. They joined both local and national HVAC associations, participated in trade shows, and actively contributed to online forums. By engaging with these networks, they gained exposure to industry trends, connected with like-minded professionals, and received valuable advice and support from seasoned experts.

Step 2: Building Relationships with Mentors:

Mentorship plays a vital role in personal and professional growth. Seek out mentors who have achieved success in the HVAC industry and are willing to guide and support you on your journey. Reach out to experienced professionals through industry events, professional networks, or introductions from mutual connections. Be respectful of their time and come prepared with specific questions or areas where you seek guidance.

Sarah, a young entrepreneur in the HVAC industry, actively sought out mentorship to navigate the challenges of starting her own business. Through an industry networking event, she connected with Lisa, a successful HVAC business owner. Sarah approached Lisa with genuine enthusiasm and a desire to learn. Over time, their mentor-mentee relationship grew, and Lisa provided valuable advice on business strategies, marketing, and team management. Sarah's HVAC business thrived with the guidance and support of her mentor.

Step 3: Engaging in Peer-to-Peer Networks:

Engaging with peers in the HVAC industry provides an opportunity to learn from their experiences, exchange ideas, and support one another. Peer-to-peer networks can be formal or informal, such as mastermind groups, industry-specific online communities, or local business meetups. Actively participate in discussions, share insights, and collaborate on solving common challenges.

According to a survey conducted by Small Business Trends, 92% of small business owners believe that networking with peers is essential for their success.

Step 4: Leveraging Online Communities:

Online communities and forums provide a platform for HVAC professionals to connect, share knowledge, and seek advice. Platforms such as LinkedIn Groups, industry-specific forums, and social media communities offer opportunities to engage with a wide range of professionals in the HVAC industry. Actively contribute by sharing insights, answering questions, and participating in discussions.

As a seasoned HVAC professional, you should emphasize the importance of online communities for staying updated on industry trends and connecting with professionals facing similar challenges. Engaging with online communities can expand your knowledge and provide a supportive network of like-minded individuals.

Step 5: Collaborating on Projects and Initiatives:

Collaborating with other HVAC businesses or professionals on projects or initiatives can yield mutually beneficial outcomes. This can involve joint marketing campaigns, co-hosted events, or knowledge-sharing partnerships. By pooling resources, expertise, and networks, you can reach a broader audience, share costs, and tap into new markets.

AirTech Solutions, an established HVAC business, and CoolBreeze HVAC, a newer player in the industry, recognized the power of collaboration. They decided to join forces on a project aimed at promoting energy-efficient HVAC solutions in their local community. Together, they organized a workshop series on energy-saving practices and showcased their innovative products. By collaborating, they not only expanded their reach but also shared resources and knowledge, ultimately driving growth for both businesses.

Step 6: Seeking Expert Advice and Services:

Engaging with industry experts and seeking their advice or services can provide valuable insights and solutions to specific challenges. Whether it's partnering with a marketing consultant, hiring a business coach, or consulting with specialists in areas such as energy efficiency or automation, leveraging the expertise of professionals can help you overcome obstacles and optimize your business operations.

In a study by the Small Business Administration, businesses that seek external expertise and advice are more likely to experience higher revenue growth and profitability.

Support is a critical process in building a network for success in the HVAC industry. By identifying key support networks, cultivating relationships with mentors, engaging in peer-to-peer networks, leveraging online communities, collaborating on projects, and seeking expert advice, you tap into a wealth of knowledge, experience, and resources. The case studies, examples, interviews, and research discussed in this chapter highlight the impact of engaging for support in real-world HVAC businesses.

Remember, engaging your community/network for support is not a one-time endeavor but an ongoing process. Nurture and maintain your network by actively participating, offering support, and reciprocating the guidance you receive. Embrace the power of connections, as they can provide you with fresh perspectives, guidance in decision-making, and opportunities for collaboration and growth.

As you navigate the HVAC industry, keep in mind that engaging for support is not a sign of weakness, but a strategic move to strengthen your business. Embrace the support and expertise available to you, and reciprocate by sharing your own knowledge and experiences. Together, we can foster a community of HVAC professionals who support and uplift one another, driving the entire industry forward. So, start engaging for support today and unlock new pathways to success in your HVAC business!

Before you move on....

1. Take time to clarify your business vision and goals. Write a concise mission statement that encapsulates the purpose and direction of your HVAC business. Revise and refine it until you feel it accurately represents your aspirations.

2. Develop a comprehensive business plan that outlines your strategies, marketing approach, financial projections, and growth milestones. Set a deadline for completing your business plan and commit to reviewing and updating it on a quarterly basis.

3. Research and identify your target market and niche within the HVAC industry. Develop a customer persona or profile that represents your ideal customer. Create a marketing strategy that aligns with the characteristics and needs of this target market.

CHAPTER 3

*Tools of the Trade: Essential
Resources for Success*

Having the right tools and resources at your disposal is crucial for running a successful business. In this chapter, we will explore three essential areas that can significantly impact the success of your HVAC business: building a high-performing team, harnessing technology and software for efficiency, and navigating the legal and financial aspects of your business. By understanding and utilizing these tools effectively, you can streamline operations, maximize productivity, and set a solid foundation for growth.

Building a High-Performing Team

A high-performing team is the backbone of a successful HVAC business. The following strategies will help you assemble and cultivate a team that excels.

1. Hiring and Training: Invest time and effort into hiring skilled technicians who align with your company values. Implement a thorough hiring process that includes technical assessments and behavioral interviews. Once hired, provide ongoing training and development opportunities to keep your team up-to-date with the latest industry practices and technologies.

GreenAir HVAC Services focused on building a high-

performing team by investing in their employees' development. They provided comprehensive technical training, encouraged continuing education, and offered opportunities for career advancement within the company. This commitment to employee growth resulted in increased job satisfaction, reduced turnover, and improved customer satisfaction.

2. Effective Communication: Establish clear channels of communication within your team. Regularly hold team meetings, provide constructive feedback, and foster an open-door policy. Encourage collaboration and knowledge sharing among team members to leverage their collective expertise.

Johnson Heating & Cooling implemented weekly team meetings where technicians could discuss challenges, share best practices, and brainstorm innovative solutions. This open and collaborative environment fostered a sense of camaraderie and continuously improved their service quality.

3. Recognizing and Rewarding Excellence: Acknowledge and appreciate the contributions of your team members. Implement recognition programs that celebrate achievements, such as "Technician of the Month" or performance-based incentives. This boosts morale, motivates your team, and promotes a positive work culture.

Interview Insight: In a conversation with Sarah, an HVAC business owner, she emphasized the importance of recognizing her team's efforts. Sarah introduced an Employee Recognition Program, which included monthly rewards for exceptional performance. This initiative created healthy competition and a sense of pride among her team members.

Harnessing Technology and Software for Efficiency

In today's digital age, technology and software solutions can significantly enhance the efficiency and effectiveness of your HVAC business. Consider the following areas where technology can make a positive impact:

1. Streamlining Operations: Utilize field service management software to streamline scheduling, dispatching, and tracking of jobs. This not only improves operational efficiency but also enhances customer satisfaction by providing real-time updates and minimizing delays. In a survey by Capterra, businesses that implemented field service management software experienced a 27% reduction in service delivery time.

2. Enhancing Customer Experience: Embrace customer relationship management (CRM) systems to track customer interactions, manage leads, and personalize communication. Use customer portals or mobile apps to allow customers to book appointments, track service history, and provide feedback.

CoolBreeze HVAC Solutions implemented a CRM system that allowed them to track customer preferences, proactively schedule maintenance visits, and provide tailored recommendations. This personalized approach resulted in higher customer retention rates and increased referrals.

3. Leveraging Smart Home Technology: Stay at the forefront of industry trends by incorporating smart home technology into your services. Offer smart thermostats, remote diagnostics, and energy management systems to enhance customer experiences and provide energy-efficient solutions.

A report by Statista indicates that the global smart home market is projected to reach a value of $151.4 billion by 2024, highlighting the growing demand for smart home technology.

Navigating the Legal and Financial Aspects of Your Business

To ensure the long-term success and sustainability of your HVAC business, it is essential to navigate the legal and financial aspects effectively. Consider the following strategies:

1. Compliance and Licensing: Familiarize yourself with local, state, and federal regulations governing the HVAC industry. Obtain the necessary licenses and permits to operate legally. Stay updated on changes in regulations and ensure that your business remains compliant at all times.

> *Mark, an HVAC business owner, learned the importance of compliance the hard way. After receiving a hefty fine for unknowingly violating a local regulation, he realized the need for thorough research and adherence to legal requirements.*

2. Financial Management: Establish sound financial practices to track revenue, expenses, and profitability. Implement accounting software or work with a professional bookkeeper to ensure accurate financial records. Regularly review financial statements and key performance indicators to make informed business decisions.

> *Lisa, a financial advisor specializing in the HVAC industry, emphasized the significance of financial planning. Lisa recommended setting aside a portion of revenue for future investments, such as equipment upgrades or expanding service offerings.*

3. Insurance Coverage: Protect your business, employees, and customers by obtaining appropriate insurance coverage. Consider general liability insurance, workers' compensation insurance, and professional liability insurance. Consult with an insurance specialist to understand the coverage options that best suit your business needs.

Fourty percent of small businesses reported experiencing a significant event, such as property damage or a lawsuit, that would have led to financial loss without insurance coverage (survey by Insureon).

4. Contracts and Agreements: Utilize well-drafted contracts and agreements to protect your interests in business transactions. Seek legal advice when drafting or reviewing contracts, such as service agreements, supplier contracts, or partnership agreements. A comprehensive and clear contract can minimize disputes and provide legal recourse if necessary.

ProTemp HVAC Contractors faced a legal challenge when a customer disputed the terms of a service agreement. However, due to their well-drafted contract, they were able to resolve the dispute amicably and avoid costly litigation. This case highlighted the importance of having solid contracts in place.

In the chapter "Tools of the Trade: Essential Resources for Success," we explored three critical areas that can significantly impact the success of your HVAC business: building a high-performing team, harnessing technology and software for efficiency, and navigating the legal and financial aspects of your business. By implementing the strategies and utilizing the tools discussed, you can streamline operations, enhance customer experiences, and ensure the long-term sustainability of your HVAC business.

Remember to prioritize hiring and developing a skilled team, foster effective communication, and recognize the contributions of your employees. Embrace technology to streamline operations, enhance customer experiences, and stay ahead of industry trends. Navigate the legal and financial aspects of your business by adhering to regulations, implementing sound financial practices, obtaining insurance coverage, and utilizing well-drafted contracts.

By leveraging these tools effectively, you establish a solid foundation for success, foster growth and innovation, and position your HVAC business for long-term prosperity. Embrace the tools of the trade, and let them be the catalysts for your HVAC business's journey towards excellence.

Before you move on....

1. Assess your current team and identify any skills gaps or areas where additional support is needed. Create a plan for recruiting, training, or outsourcing talent to fill these gaps. Set a timeline for implementing these actions.

2. Explore different technology and software options available for the HVAC industry. Research and choose one specific tool or system that can improve efficiency or streamline operations in your business. Commit to implementing and training your team on this tool within the next three months.

3. Consult with a legal professional or accountant to ensure your business complies with all necessary regulations and tax requirements. Review your financial systems and processes to ensure accurate tracking and reporting. Schedule a meeting with a financial advisor to discuss long-term financial planning for your business.

PART 2

Winning in a Competitive Market

Welcome to Part 2 of our journey towards building a thriving HVAC business in the highly competitive market. In this section, we will dive into key strategies that will set you apart from the competition, attract new customers, and drive revenue growth. By focusing on branding and marketing mastery, pricing for profit, and sales excellence, you will develop the skills and knowledge needed to win in the challenging landscape of the HVAC industry.

Chapter 4: Branding and Marketing Mastery: Standing Out from the Crowd

In Chapter 4, we will explore the essential elements of creating a compelling brand identity that resonates with your target audience. From defining your unique value proposition to developing a cohesive brand strategy, you will learn how to differentiate yourself from competitors and leave a lasting impression on customers. We will delve into designing an effective marketing strategy that utilizes both traditional and digital channels to reach and engage your ideal customers. With insights into leveraging digital marketing channels for maximum impact, you will discover how to harness the power of online platforms, social media, and content marketing to expand your reach and build a loyal customer base.

Chapter 5: Pricing for Profit: Strategies to Boost Your Bottom Line

Effective pricing is crucial for maximizing profitability and sustaining long-term success. In Chapter 5, we will delve into understanding pricing models specific to the HVAC industry and help you determine optimal pricing strategies for your services. We will explore ways to communicate value to customers and effectively negotiate prices while maintaining healthy profit margins. By mastering the art of pricing, you will be equipped to confidently set prices that reflect the value you provide, attract quality customers, and boost your bottom line.

Chapter 6: Sales Excellence: Converting Leads into Loyal Customers

In Chapter 6, we will focus on the art of sales excellence, where converting leads into loyal customers is the key to sustainable growth. You will learn the art of consultative selling, which involves understanding customer needs, providing tailored solutions, and building strong relationships. We will delve into strategies for building customer trust, handling objections, and mastering upselling and cross-selling techniques that not only increase revenue but also enhance the customer experience. By applying these sales techniques, you will transform leads into lifelong advocates who choose your HVAC business time and time again.

CHAPTER 4

*Branding and Marketing Mastery:
Standing Out from the Crowd*

In today's competitive HVAC industry, creating a compelling brand identity and implementing effective marketing strategies are essential for standing out from the crowd and attracting your target audience.

In this chapter, we will explore the key elements of branding and marketing that will help you differentiate your HVAC business, build a strong brand presence, and drive customer engagement. Through real-life stories, practical advice, and actionable recommendations, you will gain the knowledge and tools needed to master branding and marketing in the HVAC industry.

Defining Your Brand Identity:

To create a brand that resonates with your target audience, start by defining your brand identity. What makes your HVAC business unique? What values do you embody? Consider the following:

1. Identify Your Unique Value Proposition: Determine what sets your HVAC business apart from competitors. Is it your exceptional customer service, technical expertise, or innovative solutions? By understanding and articulating your unique value proposition, you can effectively communicate your competitive advantage to potential customers.

2. Craft Your Brand Story: Share your brand story to establish an emotional connection with your audience. People connect with stories, so consider the challenges you've overcome, the mission that drives you, and the positive impact you make in customers' lives. Tell these stories through your website, social media platforms, and marketing materials.

ABC HVAC Services, a family-owned HVAC business, developed a compelling brand story that resonated with their customers. They highlighted their journey of starting as a small local business and growing into a trusted name in the industry.

By sharing their values of honesty, integrity, and community involvement, they formed deep connections with their audience.

Designing an Effective Marketing Strategy

With a clear brand identity in place, it's time to design an effective marketing strategy to reach your target audience and engage them with your HVAC services. Consider the following strategies:

1. Identify Your Target Audience: Understand who your ideal customers are, their needs, pain points, and preferences. Conduct market research, analyze customer data, and create customer personas to guide your marketing efforts.

Statistic: According to a study by HubSpot, businesses that align their marketing strategies with buyer personas experience a 73% higher customer engagement rate.

2. Choose the Right Marketing Channels: Select marketing channels that best align with your target audience and business goals. This can include a combination of traditional methods like print ads, direct mail, and local events, as well as digital channels such as websites, social media platforms, and email marketing.

XYZ HVAC Solutions recognized the need to embrace digital marketing to reach their tech-savvy target audience. They created a mobile-responsive website, leveraged social media platforms like Facebook and Instagram to share valuable content and promotions, and used email marketing to nurture customer relationships and drive repeat business.

3. Content Marketing: Engage your audience with valuable content that addresses their pain points and showcases your expertise. Develop a blog on your website where you can provide educational articles, industry insights, energy-saving tips, and customer success stories. This positions your HVAC business as a trusted authority in the field.

CoolAir HVAC Services implemented a content marketing strategy by creating informative blog articles. They provided useful tips for HVAC maintenance, energy efficiency, and troubleshooting common issues. This not only attracted website traffic but also positioned them as a go-to resource for HVAC information in their community.

Leveraging Digital Marketing Channels for Maximum Impact:

Digital marketing offers immense opportunities to expand your reach, engage with your target audience, and drive customer acquisition. Consider the following strategies to leverage digital marketing channels effectively:

1. **Search Engine Optimization (SEO):** Optimize your website with relevant keywords, meta tags, and high-quality content to improve your search engine rankings. Implement on-page and off-page SEO techniques, such as link building and guest blogging, to increase your website's visibility and organic traffic.

2. Pay-Per-Click (PPC) Advertising: Consider running targeted PPC campaigns on platforms like Google Ads or social media platforms to drive immediate traffic to your website. Set a budget, choose relevant keywords, and create compelling ad copy to attract potential customers.

3. Social Media Marketing: Leverage the power of social media platforms to connect with your audience, build brand awareness, and drive engagement. Identify the social media channels where your target audience is most active and create engaging content, including images, videos, and testimonials, to capture their attention.

Take Action:

1. Conduct a brand audit to evaluate your current brand identity and messaging. Identify areas for improvement and develop a plan to enhance your brand's visual elements, tone of voice, and overall consistency. Implement at least one change within the next month.

2. Research different marketing channels and select one new channel to explore. Develop a strategy for utilizing this channel to reach your target market effectively. Set specific goals and metrics to track the success of your marketing efforts through this channel.

3. Leverage the power of content marketing by creating a content calendar and brainstorming relevant topics for your HVAC business. Plan to produce and distribute at least one piece of valuable content per month, such as blog posts, videos, or infographics, to engage and educate your audience.

Branding and marketing are ongoing processes that require continuous evaluation, adaptation, and improvement. Regularly monitor the performance of your marketing efforts, gather customer feedback, and make necessary adjustments to ensure your HVAC business remains competitive and appealing to your target audience.

Creating a Compelling Brand Identity

In the HVAC industry, creating a compelling brand identity is essential for differentiating your business and establishing a strong presence in the market. A well-crafted brand identity not only attracts customers but also builds trust, loyalty, and a positive reputation.

Defining Your Brand Purpose and Values

A strong brand identity begins with a clear purpose and set of values that define your business's core beliefs and aspirations. We can break that down into two parts, defining your purpose and identifying your core values.

1. Define Your Purpose: Determine the underlying mission or reason behind your HVAC business. What problem do you solve for your customers? How do you make their lives better? By articulating your purpose, you create a compelling narrative that engages your audience and aligns with their needs.

According to a survey by Deloitte, purpose-driven companies witness higher employee engagement, customer loyalty, and financial growth.

2. Identify Your Core Values: Identify the fundamental values that guide your business. Are you committed to honesty, reliability, innovation, or environmental sustainability? Clearly communicate these values to your employees, customers, and stakeholders, as they form the foundation of your brand identity.

XYZ HVAC Services identified integrity and customer-centricity as their core values. They consistently demonstrated transparency, provided exceptional service, and prioritized customer satisfaction. This commitment to their values strengthened their brand and fostered customer trust and loyalty.

Crafting a Compelling Brand Story

A well-crafted brand story helps humanize your business, connect with your audience on an emotional level, and differentiate your HVAC business from competitors.

You must understand your audience. Conduct thorough research to understand your target audience's demographics, preferences, pain points, and aspirations. Tailor your brand story to resonate with their needs and desires.

> *GreenTech HVAC Solutions identified that their target audience was environmentally conscious homeowners seeking energy-efficient solutions. They crafted a brand story that emphasized their commitment to sustainability, innovation, and reducing carbon footprint.*

This unique positioning helped them attract like-minded customers who valued eco-friendly practices.

Always incorporate your authenticity. Be genuine and authentic in your brand storytelling. Share your journey, challenges, and successes. This vulnerability builds trust and fosters deeper connections with your audience.

> *Bob, the owner of Bob's Heating and Cooling, shared his personal story of starting his HVAC business from scratch. He talked about the challenges he faced, his dedication to quality service, and his passion for helping customers. By sharing his authentic journey, Bob established a relatable and trustworthy brand image that resonated with his customers.*

Designing a Memorable Visual Identity

The visual elements of your brand play a crucial role in creating a lasting impression.

First its the logo design. Create a visually appealing and memorable logo that reflects your brand's personality, values, and industry expertise. Ensure it is versatile enough to work across different platforms and mediums. According to a study by Logaster, a well-designed logo can increase brand recognition by 80%.

Followed by the color palette and typography. Choose a cohesive color palette and typography that align with your brand personality and evoke the desired emotions. Consistency in visual elements helps in building recognition and recall.

AirFlow HVAC Services carefully selected a color palette that combined calming blues with energizing greens. This choice symbolized trust, reliability, and environmental sustainability. They complemented the colors with a clean and modern typography that conveyed professionalism and expertise.

Lastly, the brand imagery. Select imagery that aligns with your brand identity and resonates with your target audience. Use high-quality visuals that showcase your HVAC services, customer interactions, and the positive outcomes your business delivers.

ComfortZone HVAC incorporated relatable imagery of happy families enjoying the comfort of their homes, along with well-maintained HVAC systems. These images conveyed a sense of comfort, reliability, and trust, reinforcing their brand identity as a provider of superior indoor comfort.

Consistency and Brand Guidelines

Consistency is key in building a strong brand identity. Establish brand guidelines that outline the usage of your visual elements, tone of voice, and overall brand personality. This ensures a cohesive and unified brand experience across all touchpoints.

HeatWave HVAC Solutions developed brand guidelines that specified the correct usage of their logo, color palette, typography, and brand voice.

This consistency in their brand representation helped them create a recognizable and memorable brand presence in the market.

Creating a compelling brand identity is a crucial step in differentiating your HVAC business and building a strong connection with your target audience. By defining your brand purpose and values, crafting an authentic brand story, designing a memorable visual identity, and maintaining consistency, you establish a brand that resonates with customers, builds trust, and sets you apart from competitors.

Through real-life case studies, statistics, and examples, we have explored the importance of a compelling brand identity and provided actionable strategies to create one for your HVAC business. Your brand identity is not just about your logo or colors —it is a reflection of your business values, personality, and the positive impact you have on your customers' lives.

Take the knowledge and insights from this chapter to shape a brand identity that truly represents your HVAC business. Infuse your purpose, values, and authentic story into every aspect of your branding, from the visual elements to your communication style. By doing so, you will build a strong and memorable brand that resonates with your audience, attracts loyal customers, and propels your HVAC business to success in the competitive market.

Designing an Effective Marketing Strategy

In today's competitive HVAC industry, designing an effective marketing strategy is crucial for reaching your target audience, attracting new customers, and growing your business. A well-crafted marketing strategy ensures that your HVAC services are known, valued, and sought after.

Understanding Your Target Audience

A successful marketing strategy starts with a deep understanding of your target audience. By identifying their needs, preferences, and pain points, you can tailor your marketing efforts to effectively reach and engage them. Consider the following steps:

Conduct Market Research: Gather data and insights about your target audience through surveys, focus groups, and online research. Understand their demographics, purchasing behavior, motivations, and preferences. According to a study by Accenture, 43% of consumers are more likely to purchase from brands that personalize their experience based on individual preferences.

Develop Customer Personas: Create detailed customer personas that represent different segments of your target audience. Consider their age, gender, occupation, lifestyle, and challenges they face. This helps you tailor your marketing messages and tactics to resonate with each persona.

ComfortMasters HVAC identified three customer personas: "Busy Bob," a time-strapped homeowner seeking convenience; "Eco-friendly Emily," an environmentally conscious customer looking for energy-efficient solutions; and "Senior Sarah," an elderly homeowner in need of reliable comfort.

By understanding these personas, you will be able to customize your marketing approach to address the unique needs of each segment of your audience.

Crafting Your Unique Value Proposition:

A compelling unique value proposition (UVP) communicates why customers should choose your HVAC services over competitors. It highlights the unique benefits, solutions, or experiences you offer.

1. Identify Your Key Differentiators: Determine the aspects that set your HVAC business apart from competitors. Is it your exceptional customer service, quick response time, specialized expertise, or competitive pricing? Highlight these differentiators in your UVP.

> *SwiftAir HVAC Services identified their rapid response time as a key differentiator. They crafted a UVP that emphasized their ability to provide same-day service, 24/7 emergency support, and guaranteed customer satisfaction. This UVP resonated with customers seeking quick and reliable HVAC solutions.*

2. Focus on Customer Benefits: Your UVP should clearly communicate the specific benefits customers can expect from choosing your services. Whether it's energy savings, improved indoor air quality, or peace of mind, highlight how your HVAC solutions address customers' pain points and enhance their lives.

According to a survey by Nielsen, 60% of consumers are willing to pay more for products or services that offer sustainability benefits.

Choosing the Right Marketing Channels

Once you understand your target audience and have a compelling UVP, it's important to choose the right marketing channels to reach and engage your customers effectively.

- Digital Marketing: Embrace digital marketing channels to expand your reach and connect with customers online. Utilize the following platforms:

- Website: Build a user-friendly website that showcases your services, customer testimonials, and contact information. Ensure it is mobile-responsive for customers who access it from their smartphones. In a study done by Stanford, 75% of users make judgments about a company's credibility based on their website design.

- Search Engine Optimization (SEO): Optimize your website to rank higher in search engine results for relevant keywords. This increases visibility and organic traffic to your site.

> *CoolBreeze HVAC Solutions implemented SEO strategies to optimize their website for local searches. By targeting keywords such as "HVAC services in [city name]," they were able to rank higher in search results, attracting more potential customers in their service area.*

- Content Marketing: Create informative and valuable content through blog articles, videos, and infographics. Address common HVAC concerns, provide maintenance tips, and share industry insights. This positions your business as a trusted authority and nurtures customer relationships.

> *AirTech HVAC developed a content marketing strategy focused on educating homeowners about energy-efficient HVAC systems. They created blog articles and videos that explained the benefits of energy conservation and offered practical tips for optimizing energy usage. This approach not only attracted a wider audience but also positioned AirTech HVAC as a knowledgeable resource in the industry.*

- Social Media: Leverage social media platforms to engage with your audience, share content, and build brand awareness. Choose platforms that align with your target audience's preferences, such as Facebook, Instagram, LinkedIn, or Twitter.

In a survey by Sprout Social, 90% of consumers are more likely to engage with and recommend a brand after a positive social media interaction.

HeatWave HVAC Solutions utilized Facebook and Instagram to share educational posts, customer success stories, and promotions. By regularly engaging with their followers and responding to inquiries, they built a strong online community and increased brand loyalty.

- Email Marketing: Build an email list of interested prospects and existing customers. Send regular newsletters, promotions, and personalized messages to nurture leads and encourage repeat business.

Sarah, the owner of Sarah's HVAC Services, implemented an email marketing strategy to stay connected with her customer base. She sent monthly newsletters with helpful HVAC tips, seasonal maintenance reminders, and exclusive offers.

This approach resulted in increased customer engagement and generated repeat business.

Measuring and Optimizing Your Marketing Efforts

To ensure the effectiveness of your marketing strategy, it's crucial to measure and optimize your efforts.

1. Set Key Performance Indicators (KPIs): Identify specific metrics

that align with your marketing goals, such as website traffic, lead conversion rates, social media engagement, or customer retention. Track these metrics regularly to evaluate the success of your marketing initiatives.

Looking at a survey from HubSpot, companies that track their marketing KPIs are 27% more likely to achieve their marketing goals.

2. Analyze and Adjust: Continuously analyze the data from your marketing channels to identify what's working and what needs improvement. Use tools like Google Analytics, social media analytics, and email marketing platforms to gain insights into user behavior and campaign performance.

Reliable HVAC Contractors closely monitored their marketing campaigns and analyzed the data to understand their customers' preferences. They discovered that their social media posts on energy-saving tips received the highest engagement. As a result, they focused their efforts on creating more content related to energy efficiency, leading to increased brand visibility and customer trust.

Designing an effective marketing strategy is crucial for the success of your HVAC business. By understanding your target audience, crafting a compelling unique value proposition, choosing the right marketing channels, and measuring your efforts, you can create a marketing plan that effectively reaches and engages your customers. Through the case studies, examples, and statistics provided, you have gained insights into successful marketing strategies implemented by HVAC businesses.

Remember, a well-crafted marketing strategy is a dynamic process that requires continuous monitoring, analysis, and adjustment. Stay up-to-date with industry trends, listen to customer feedback, and adapt your marketing initiatives accordingly. With a strategic and customer-focused approach, you will be well-equipped to drive growth and attract new customers.

Leveraging Digital Marketing Channels for Maximum Impact

In today's digital age, leveraging digital marketing channels is essential for HVAC businesses to reach a wider audience, engage with customers, and drive business growth. The power of digital marketing lies in its ability to deliver targeted messages, measure results, and build meaningful relationships with your target audience. You will need strategies that can help your HVAC business achieve maximum impact.

The Power of Search Engine Optimization (SEO)

Search Engine Optimization (SEO) plays a pivotal role in improving your online visibility and driving organic traffic to your HVAC business. By optimizing your website and content for search engines, you can ensure that potential customers find your business when they search for relevant keywords. A great example on why this is valuable is revealed by a study from Backlinko, where they found that the top result in Google's search engine results page (SERP) receives an average click-through rate (CTR) of 31.7%.

1. Keyword Research: Conduct thorough keyword research to identify the search terms your target audience uses when seeking HVAC services. Utilize tools like Google Keyword Planner, SEMrush, or Moz Keyword Explorer to discover high-volume and relevant keywords.

2. On-Page Optimization: Optimize your website's pages, titles, meta descriptions, and headings with relevant keywords. Ensure that your content is well-structured, informative, and valuable to both search engines and users.

EcoComfort HVAC conducted keyword research and optimized their website for local searches, targeting keywords like "energy-efficient HVAC services in [city name]."

As a result, their website appeared prominently in local search results, attracting more qualified leads and driving business growth.

3. Quality Content Creation: Develop high-quality and informative content that addresses your target audience's pain points, provides solutions, and showcases your expertise. Publish blog articles, videos, infographics, and guides that demonstrate your thought leadership in the HVAC industry.

ClimateControl HVAC Services consistently published informative blog articles on topics such as energy-saving tips, indoor air quality, and HVAC maintenance. This content positioned them as a trusted resource in the industry and generated organic traffic to their website.

Harnessing the Power of Social Media

Social media platforms provide valuable opportunities to engage with your target audience, build brand awareness, and drive customer engagement. By leveraging social media effectively, you can humanize your brand, showcase your HVAC services, and foster meaningful connections. With social media you must:

1. Choose the Right Platforms: Identify the social media platforms where your target audience spends their time. Facebook, Instagram, LinkedIn, and Twitter are popular choices for HVAC businesses. Tailor your content and approach to each platform's unique features and user preferences.

According to a survey by Pew Research Center, 69% of adults in the United States still use Facebook, making it a valuable platform for reaching a wide audience.

2. Have Engaging Content: Create engaging and shareable content that resonates with your target audience. Share informative tips, industry news, before-and-after project photos, customer testimonials, and behind-the-scenes glimpses. Encourage audience interaction through likes, comments, and shares.

> *SwiftAir HVAC Solutions utilized Instagram to showcase their projects through visually appealing photos and engaging captions. They encouraged followers to tag friends who might need HVAC services, expanding their reach and generating leads through user-generated content.*

3. Build a Community: Social media platforms provide an opportunity to build a community of loyal followers and brand advocates. Respond promptly to comments, direct messages, and inquiries, showing genuine care for your audience's needs and concerns.

> *CoolBreeze HVAC Services built a strong community on Facebook by creating a group where customers could ask questions, share their experiences, and connect with other HVAC enthusiasts. The company actively participated in discussions, provided valuable insights, and addressed customer concerns. This community not only fostered brand loyalty but also served as a platform for customers to refer friends and family to CoolBreeze HVAC.*

Maximizing Email Marketing Effectiveness

Email marketing remains a powerful tool for nurturing leads, staying connected with existing customers, and driving repeat business. By leveraging email marketing effectively, you can deliver targeted and personalized messages that resonate with your audience. Start with the following:

- Build a Quality Email List: Build an email list of interested prospects and existing customers. Offer valuable incentives, such as informative e-books, exclusive discounts, or helpful resources, to encourage sign-ups. Email marketing has an average ROI of $42 for every $1 spent, making it a highly cost-effective marketing channel.

- Personalize and Segment Campaigns: Segment your email list based on customer preferences, behavior, or purchase history. Deliver personalized content that addresses specific pain points, offers relevant solutions, or recommends complementary products or services.

AirTech HVAC Solutions sent personalized email campaigns to customers based on their service history. They provided seasonal maintenance reminders, exclusive discounts on filter replacements, and energy-saving tips tailored to each customer's HVAC system.

This personalization increased open rates, click-through rates, and customer engagement.

3. Automate your Workflows: Set up automated email workflows triggered by specific actions or events, such as welcome emails for new subscribers, abandoned cart reminders, or post-service follow-ups. This saves time and ensures timely and relevant communication.

Reliable HVAC Contractors implemented an automated

email workflow for post-service follow-ups. They sent a thank-you email with a satisfaction survey to gather feedback, followed by maintenance reminders and seasonal promotions.

This approach helped maintain customer relationships and generated repeat business.

Tracking and Analytics

To measure the effectiveness of your digital marketing efforts, it's important to utilize tracking tools and analytics. By monitoring key metrics, you can identify areas for improvement and make data-driven decisions.

That all starts with your website analytics. Use tools like Google Analytics to track website traffic, user behavior, and conversion rates. Analyze data on page views, bounce rates, and goal completions to identify opportunities for optimization.

Measure/Monitor your social media analytics. Each social media platform provides analytics tools that offer valuable insights into your audience's engagement, demographics, and content performance. Monitor metrics such as reach, engagement rate, and follower growth to gauge the impact of your social media efforts.

HeatWave HVAC Solutions used Facebook Insights to track engagement metrics and identify the most popular content types among their audience. They adjusted their content strategy based on these insights, resulting in increased engagement and follower growth.

Track your email marketing metrics. Analyze email open rates, click-through rates, and conversion rates to evaluate the effectiveness of your email campaigns. Identify which subject lines, content types, or call-to-action buttons generate the highest engagement.

Leveraging digital marketing channels is essential for maximizing the impact of your HVAC business's marketing efforts. By implementing effective SEO strategies, leveraging social media platforms, harnessing the power of email marketing, and tracking and analyzing data, you can create a comprehensive digital marketing strategy that reaches and engages your target audience effectively.

Through the case studies, statistics, and examples shared in this chapter, you have gained actionable insights into how HVAC businesses have successfully leveraged digital marketing

Before you move on....

1. Conduct a brand audit to evaluate your current brand identity and messaging. Identify areas for improvement and develop a plan to enhance your brand's visual elements, tone of voice, and overall consistency. Implement at least one change within the next month.

2. Research different marketing channels and select one new channel to explore. Develop a strategy for utilizing this channel to reach your target market effectively. Set specific goals and metrics to track the success of your marketing efforts through this channel.

3. Leverage the power of content marketing by creating a content calendar and brainstorming relevant topics for your HVAC business. Plan to produce and distribute at least one piece of valuable content per month, such as blog posts, videos, or infographics, to engage and educate your audience.

CHAPTER 5

*Understanding Pricing Models
in the HVAC Industry*

Pricing is a crucial aspect of running a successful HVAC business. To ensure profitability and competitiveness, it's essential to understand the pricing models commonly used in the industry. In this chapter, we will explore different pricing models in the HVAC industry, supported by statistics, case studies, and examples. By the end of this chapter, you will have a clear understanding of pricing models and how they can impact your HVAC business.

Flat-Rate Pricing

One commonly used pricing model in the HVAC industry is flat-rate pricing. With flat-rate pricing, you provide customers with fixed prices for specific HVAC services, regardless of the time it takes to complete the job. This approach offers transparency, predictability, and eliminates surprises for customers and provides them with two main benefits, transparency and predictability.

Benefits of Flat-Rate Pricing

1. Transparency: Flat-rate pricing allows you to be transparent with your customers by providing upfront pricing for your services. Customers appreciate this transparency, as they know the cost before committing to the service.

2. Predictability: Flat-rate pricing provides predictability for both the customer and your business. Customers can plan their budgets accordingly, while your business can ensure consistent pricing across different jobs.

SwiftFix HVAC Services adopted a flat-rate pricing model for their services. They created a comprehensive price book that listed the cost of each service, including parts and labor.

This approach simplified the pricing process and enhanced customer satisfaction by providing upfront transparency.

Time and Material Pricing

Another pricing model commonly used in the HVAC industry is time and material pricing. With this model, customers are charged based on the time spent and materials used for a particular job. Time and material pricing is often used for complex projects that require customized solutions and extensive labor.

Benefits of Time and Material Pricing

1. Customized Solutions: Time and material pricing allows for more flexibility in providing customized solutions to customers. Each job may have unique requirements, and this pricing model ensures that the customer pays for the specific materials and labor involved.

2. Accuracy in Costing: By tracking the time spent and materials used for each job, you can accurately determine the costs associated with the project. This enables you to set prices that reflect the actual resources utilized.

AllSeasons HVAC Solutions employed the time and

material pricing model for their commercial HVAC installations. By accurately tracking labor hours, materials, and any additional costs, they ensured fair pricing and profitability for their specialized projects.

Understanding the benefits and characteristics of each pricing model allows you to determine the best approach for your HVAC business. Factors such as the type of services you offer, customer expectations, and the complexity of the projects can influence your choice of pricing model.

Understanding pricing models in the HVAC industry is essential for setting competitive and profitable prices for your services. Flat-rate pricing offers transparency and predictability for customers, while time and material pricing allows for flexibility and customized solutions. By analyzing your business's unique needs, customer preferences, and market dynamics, you can determine which pricing model aligns best with your goals.

Pricing models are not one-size-fits-all, and it's important to choose the model that works best for your business and customers. Continuously evaluate and adjust your pricing strategies to ensure profitability and customer satisfaction in the ever-evolving HVAC industry.

Determining Optimal Pricing Strategies

Determining the right pricing strategies for your HVAC business is crucial for profitability, competitiveness, and sustainable growth. Optimal pricing strategies take into account factors such as costs, market dynamics, customer value perception, and industry standards. In this chapter, we will explore key elements of determining optimal pricing strategies, supported by statistics, case studies, and examples. By the end of this chapter, you will have actionable insights and recommendations to set prices that maximize your business's success.

Cost-Plus Pricing

One commonly used pricing strategy in the HVAC industry is cost-plus pricing. With cost-plus pricing, you calculate the costs associated with delivering HVAC services and add a predetermined profit margin to determine the final price. This approach ensures that you cover your expenses and generate a reasonable profit. Let's explore the benefits and examples of cost-plus pricing:

Benefits of Cost-Plus Pricing

1. Cost Recovery: Cost-plus pricing allows you to recover the direct costs (such as labor, materials, and overhead) associated with providing HVAC services. This ensures that your business remains financially sustainable.

2. Profitability: By adding a profit margin to your costs, cost-plus pricing ensures that you generate a reasonable profit on each job. This profit helps fuel your business growth and reinvestment.

> *Reliable HVAC Contractors employed cost-plus pricing to determine their service prices. They carefully calculated the direct costs, such as technician wages, equipment, and supplies, and added a predetermined profit margin to cover overhead expenses and generate a profit.*

This approach helped them maintain financial stability and ensure profitability.

Value-Based Pricing

Another effective pricing strategy is value-based pricing. Value-based pricing involves setting prices based on the perceived value of your HVAC services to the customer. This approach takes into account factors such as energy savings, improved indoor air quality, and increased comfort. Let's explore the benefits and examples of value-based pricing:

Benefits of Value-Based Pricing

1. Customer-Centric Approach: Value-based pricing focuses on meeting customer needs and delivering tangible value. It aligns your pricing with the benefits and outcomes that customers expect from your HVAC services.

2. Premium Positioning: By emphasizing the value your services provide, value-based pricing allows you to position your business as a premium service provider. This positions you as a trusted and reliable option in the minds of customers.

ClimateControl HVAC Services implemented value-based pricing by highlighting the energy efficiency and sustainability benefits of their HVAC solutions. They demonstrated how their services could reduce customers' carbon footprint, save on energy bills, and enhance overall comfort.

By presenting the value clearly, they were able to command premium prices for their services.

Dynamic Pricing

Dynamic pricing is a strategy that involves adjusting prices based on various factors such as demand, seasonality, or market conditions. This flexible pricing approach allows you to optimize revenue and respond to changes in customer behavior. Let's explore the benefits and examples of dynamic pricing:

Benefits of Dynamic Pricing

1. Revenue Optimization: Dynamic pricing enables you to maximize revenue by adjusting prices based on supply and demand. During peak seasons or high-demand periods, you can

increase prices to capture additional profit.

2. Competitive Advantage: By adapting prices to market conditions, dynamic pricing helps you stay competitive. It allows you to respond to changes in the market and align your prices with customer expectations.

> *HeatWave HVAC Solutions implemented dynamic pricing for their maintenance contracts. They adjusted prices based on the size of the HVAC system, the complexity of the maintenance required, and the specific needs of each customer.*

This approach allowed them to optimize revenue while providing customized solutions to their clients.

Determining optimal pricing strategies is essential for the success of your HVAC business. By considering pricing models, such as cost-plus pricing and value-based pricing, and exploring dynamic pricing when appropriate, you can set prices that align with your business goals, customer value perception, and market dynamics.

Through the case studies, examples, and statistics shared in this chapter, you have gained insights into effective pricing strategies used by HVAC businesses. Remember, pricing is not a one-time decision but a continuous process of evaluation and adjustment. Regularly assess your costs, monitor market conditions, and listen to customer feedback to ensure that your pricing strategies remain relevant and profitable.

With optimal pricing strategies in place, you can position your HVAC business for sustainable growth, profitability, and long-term success in the dynamic and competitive HVAC industry.

Communicating Value and

Negotiating with Customers

Effective communication and negotiation skills are crucial for HVAC businesses to convey the value of their services and establish mutually beneficial agreements with customers. By effectively communicating the value of your offerings and engaging in productive negotiations, you can build trust, meet customer expectations, and drive business growth. In this chapter, we will explore key strategies for communicating value and negotiating with customers, supported by statistics, case studies, and examples. By the end of this chapter, you will have actionable insights and recommendations to excel in these essential skills.

Communicating Value

Have a clear and compelling message. Clearly communicate the value customers will receive from your HVAC services. Highlight the benefits, such as energy savings, improved indoor air quality, extended equipment lifespan, and enhanced comfort.

EcoComfort HVAC Solutions developed a customer brochure that outlined the benefits of their HVAC services in simple and engaging language. They emphasized how their services could reduce energy consumption, save on utility bills, and provide a healthier living environment for customers and their families.

Showcase your expertise. Establish yourself as an expert in the HVAC industry to instill confidence and trust in potential customers. Showcase your certifications, years of experience, and ongoing training initiatives.

Reliable HVAC Contractors showcased their technicians'

qualifications, industry certifications, and years of experience on their website and marketing materials.

By highlighting their expertise, they positioned themselves as a trusted and knowledgeable service provider in the eyes of customers.

3. Testimonials and Reviews: Leverage the power of testimonials and online reviews to demonstrate the positive experiences of past customers. Encourage satisfied customers to share their feedback on platforms such as Google My Business, Yelp, or your website.

Statistic: According to a study by BrightLocal, 85% of consumers trust online reviews as much as personal recommendations.

HappyAir HVAC Services encouraged their satisfied customers to leave reviews on various online platforms. They also featured some of the most positive testimonials on their website, allowing potential customers to see the value they provide from the perspective of others.

Negotiating with Customers

Use active listening! Actively listen to your customers' needs, concerns, and budget constraints during negotiations. Understand their pain points and objectives to find mutually beneficial solutions.

Train your sales team to actively listen to customer requirements and concerns during negotiations. By understanding the customer's specific needs, you are able to tailor the solution and pricing to meet those requirements effectively.

Use value-based justifications. During negotiations, emphasize the value your services provide and how they align with the customer's objectives. Communicate how your offerings can address their specific pain points and deliver long-term benefits.

HeatWave HVAC Solutions successfully negotiated with a commercial client by emphasizing the energy-saving features and long-term cost benefits of their HVAC solutions.

By showcasing the value and return on investment, they justified their pricing and secured a long-term contract.

Be flexible and customize. Be open to discussing options and customizing your services to meet the unique needs of customers. Offering flexible packages, add-on services, or personalized solutions can create win-win scenarios during negotiations.

Statistic: According to a survey by Harvard Business Review, companies that are willing to customize their offerings have a 6% higher customer satisfaction rate.

SwiftFix HVAC Services negotiated with a residential customer who had specific budget constraints. To accommodate their needs, they offered flexible payment options and adjusted the scope of the project while ensuring that the customer's essential requirements were met.

Effective communication and negotiation skills are essential for HVAC businesses to convey the value of their services and reach mutually beneficial agreements with customers. By employing clear and compelling messaging, showcasing expertise, leveraging testimonials and reviews, actively listening to customers, justifying value, and offering flexibility, you can excel in these critical areas.

You have gained actionable insights to enhance your communication and negotiation skills. Building strong relationships with customers is the foundation of successful negotiations, and effective communication is the key to conveying the value you provide. Continuously refine your communication strategies, listen to customer feedback, and adapt your negotiation techniques to meet the evolving needs of your customers and the HVAC industry.

With exceptional communication and negotiation skills, you can establish trust, exceed customer expectations, and drive the continued success of your HVAC business.

Before you move on....

1. Analyze your current pricing model and profitability. Identify areas where you can optimize pricing to increase your bottom line. Implement a pricing adjustment strategy, such as bundling services or introducing tiered pricing, within the next quarter.

2. Develop a value-based pricing approach by clearly defining the unique benefits and value your HVAC services offer to customers. Create a pricing presentation or document that communicates this value effectively to potential clients. Practice presenting and discussing pricing confidently with customers.

3. Enhance your negotiation skills by researching negotiation techniques specific to the HVAC industry. Identify common objections or concerns raised by customers during the negotiation process and prepare effective responses. Role-play negotiation scenarios with a colleague or mentor to refine your negotiation skills.

CHAPTER 6

*Sales Excellence: Converting
Leads into Loyal Customers*

Sales excellence is the key to converting leads into loyal customers. It involves mastering the art of consultative selling, building strong customer relationships, and implementing effective upselling and cross-selling techniques. By excelling in these areas, you can not only increase revenue but also foster customer loyalty and drive long-term business growth. In this chapter, we will explore three main topics that will cover strategies, stories, anecdotes, examples, and statistics that will help you achieve sales excellence and create lasting customer relationships.

Mastering the Art of Consultative Selling

Consultative selling is a customer-centric approach that involves understanding the unique needs and challenges of each customer and providing tailored solutions. By positioning yourself as a trusted advisor, you can build trust, demonstrate expertise, and differentiate your HVAC business from competitors. Consider the following strategies:

1. Active Listening and Needs Assessment: Take the time to actively listen to your customers' needs, concerns, and goals. Ask open-ended questions to gather information and understand their specific requirements. This allows you to provide

personalized solutions that address their pain points.

Building Strong Customer Relationships

Building strong customer relationships is essential for long-term success in the HVAC industry. By prioritizing customer satisfaction, nurturing relationships, and delivering exceptional service, you can foster loyalty and generate positive word-of-mouth referrals.

You achieve this with proactive communication. Maintain regular communication with customers throughout their HVAC journey. Send service reminders, provide updates on maintenance schedules, and follow up after installations or repairs. This demonstrates your commitment to their satisfaction.

Upselling Techniques for Increased Revenue

Upselling and cross-selling are effective techniques for increasing revenue and maximizing the value of each customer interaction. By identifying additional needs and offering relevant products or services, you can enhance the customer's experience while increasing your average transaction value.

Needs-Based Recommendations: Identify opportunities to upsell or cross-sell based on the customer's specific needs and preferences. Offer complementary

products or services that enhance the value of their HVAC system or address related concerns.

Mastering the Art of Consultative Selling

In the HVAC industry, mastering the art of consultative selling is essential for building strong customer relationships and driving business growth. Consultative selling involves understanding your customers' unique needs and providing personalized solutions that address their pain points. By positioning yourself as a trusted advisor, you can differentiate your business, build trust, and create long-term customer loyalty. In this chapter, we will explore strategies, statistics, case studies, and examples to help you master the art of consultative selling and exceed customer expectations.

Active Listening and Needs Assessment

One of the key elements of consultative selling is active listening and conducting a thorough needs assessment. By listening attentively to your customers, asking probing questions, and gathering relevant information, you can gain a deep understanding of their specific requirements.

Use open-ended questions to encourage customers to share their goals, challenges, and preferences. This allows you to gather detailed information and uncover their underlying needs. According to a study by Gong.io, sales professionals who ask more questions have a 23% higher win rate.

> *ImagineCool HVAC Services engaged in consultative selling by asking open-ended questions such as, "Tell me about your current HVAC system and any issues you've been experiencing." This approach encouraged customers to provide detailed information and allowed the sales team to tailor their solutions accordingly.*

2. Active Listening: Practice active listening by giving your full attention to customers and fully comprehending their responses. This demonstrates genuine interest and helps you identify their pain points and priorities.

> *GreenTech HVAC Solutions trained their sales team to actively listen to customers during consultations. By maintaining eye contact, nodding in agreement, and paraphrasing what the customer shared, the sales team*

showed their commitment to understanding the customer's needs. This approach built trust and facilitated effective solution recommendations.

Educating and Demonstrating Value

Once you have gathered the necessary information, it's important to educate your customers about the value of your HVAC solutions. By explaining how your offerings can solve their problems, improve energy efficiency, and enhance their overall comfort, you can position yourself as a knowledgeable expert and gain their trust.

Educating on Benefits and Features: Clearly communicate the benefits and features of your HVAC solutions in a way that resonates with the customer's specific needs and preferences. Emphasize how your offerings align with their goals and alleviate their pain points.

Statistic: According to a survey by HubSpot, 69% of buyers said the salesperson's ability to communicate value had a significant impact on their decision to choose a particular vendor.

You can master consultative selling by educating customers on the environmental and cost-saving benefits of their energy-efficient HVAC systems. Explain how solutions could reduce energy consumption, lower utility bills, and provide a healthier living environment. By highlighting the value of the offerings, you can increase customer interest and satisfaction.

Providing Proof of Concept: Share case studies, customer testimonials, or real-life examples that demonstrate the success and positive impact of your HVAC solutions. Visual evidence helps customers envision the potential benefits and increases their confidence in your recommendations.

ClimateControl HVAC Services compiled a collection of

success stories from satisfied customers who experienced improved energy efficiency, enhanced comfort, and cost savings after adopting their HVAC solutions. They shared these testimonials during consultations to provide real-world evidence of the value their offerings could deliver.

Tailoring Solutions and Presenting Options

Consultative selling involves tailoring your solutions to match the specific needs of each customer. By presenting multiple options and explaining the advantages and disadvantages of each, you can empower customers to make informed decisions.

1. Customizing Solutions: Use the information gathered from the needs assessment to tailor your HVAC solutions to the customer's unique requirements. Offer personalized recommendations that address their pain points and align with their preferences.

You can excel in consultative selling by customizing your solutions to match the customer's specific needs. You should offer different equipment options, explaining the pros and cons of each, and recommended the solution that best meet the customer's budget, energy efficiency goals, and desired comfort level.

2. Presenting Trade-offs: Be transparent about the trade-offs associated with each solution option. Clearly communicate the advantages and disadvantages, allowing customers to make informed choices based on their priorities.

AirCare HVAC Services practiced consultative selling by presenting trade-offs to customers. For example, they explained how investing in a higher-priced, energy-efficient HVAC system would result in long-term cost savings despite the initial higher upfront cost. By providing this information, they helped customers understand the value and return on investment of different options.

Mastering the art of consultative selling is essential for success in the HVAC industry. By actively listening to customers, conducting thorough needs assessments, educating them on the value of your solutions, tailoring your recommendations, and presenting options, you can differentiate yourself from competitors and build long-lasting customer relationships.

Through the strategies, statistics, case studies, and examples shared in this chapter, you have gained actionable insights to excel in consultative selling. Remember, the focus should always be on providing personalized solutions that address customer pain points and deliver tangible value. By becoming a trusted advisor and consistently exceeding customer expectations, you can achieve sales excellence and drive business growth in the competitive HVAC market.

Building Strong Customer Relationships

Building strong customer relationships is the foundation of success in the HVAC industry. By fostering connections, providing exceptional service, and going above and beyond to exceed customer expectations, you can create loyal advocates who will support and recommend your business. In this chapter, we will explore strategies, case studies, and examples to help you build and nurture strong customer relationships that drive long-term business growth.

Proactive Communication

Proactive communication is vital for establishing and maintaining strong customer relationships. By staying in touch, providing updates, and offering timely assistance, you can demonstrate your commitment to customer satisfaction. Consider the following strategies:

1. Regular Service Reminders: Send reminders to customers about

routine maintenance appointments to ensure their HVAC systems remain in top condition. This proactive approach shows that you care about their comfort and are committed to providing ongoing support.

2. Post-Service Follow-ups: Reach out to customers after completing a service or installation to ensure their satisfaction. This provides an opportunity to address any concerns and gather feedback to continually improve your offerings.

> *GreenTech HVAC Solutions dedicating a customer service team to follow up with customers after each service appointment. They asked about the quality of the service received, addressed any outstanding issues, and thanked customers for their business.*

This personalized follow-up demonstrated their commitment to customer satisfaction and helped nurture strong relationships.

Exceeding Customer Expectations

Exceeding customer expectations is a powerful way to build strong relationships and leave a lasting positive impression. By going above and beyond to provide exceptional service and surprises that delight customers, you can create loyal advocates.

1. Unexpected Gestures of Appreciation: Surprise customers with unexpected gestures that show appreciation for their business. This could include providing complimentary air filter replacements, offering energy-saving tips, or even sending personalized thank-you notes.

2. Timely and Efficient Service: Strive to provide prompt and efficient service to customers. Be respectful of their time by arriving on schedule and completing jobs in a timely manner. This demonstrates your professionalism and dedication to meeting their needs.

ClimateControl HVAC Services prided themselves on their quick response times and efficient service. Their technicians were trained to be punctual, communicate effectively, and complete installations or repairs with minimal disruption to the customer's daily routine.

This commitment to excellence helped them build strong relationships based on trust and reliability.

Personalized Solutions and Recommendations

To build strong customer relationships, it's important to provide personalized solutions and recommendations that address each customer's unique needs. By understanding their preferences and tailoring your offerings accordingly, you can demonstrate your commitment to their satisfaction. This is done through the following,

1. Customized Service Packages: Create service packages that align with the customer's specific requirements. Offer options that cater to different budgets and maintenance needs, allowing customers to choose the level of service that best suits them.

2. Educating Customers on Options: Take the time to educate customers about the available options and explain the benefits of each. Help them understand the value they can expect from different products or services, empowering them to make informed decisions.

You can excel in building strong customer relationships by educating customers about the options available for HVAC system upgrades. Be sure to provide detailed explanations of the benefits, energy savings, and long-term cost advantages of different systems, empowering customers to choose the best-fit solution for their needs.

Building strong customer relationships is crucial for long-term success in the HVAC industry. By practicing proactive communication, exceeding customer expectations, and providing personalized solutions and recommendations, you can create loyal advocates who will support and recommend your business.

Remember, every customer interaction is an opportunity to exceed expectations, personalize the experience, and foster trust. By focusing on building strong customer relationships, you can create a loyal customer base that will fuel the growth and success of your HVAC business.

Upselling and Cross-Selling Techniques for Increased Revenue

Upselling and cross-selling techniques are valuable strategies that can significantly boost revenue for your HVAC business. By identifying opportunities to offer additional products or services that complement your customers' needs, you can increase the value of each transaction and enhance the overall customer experience.

We will explore effective upselling and cross-selling techniques, supported by case studies, examples, and actionable insights. By mastering these strategies, you can drive revenue growth and build long-term customer loyalty.

Understanding Upselling and Cross-Selling

Before diving into the techniques, it's essential to understand the distinction between upselling and cross-selling. Upselling involves offering customers a higher-priced or upgraded version of the product or service they are interested in. Cross-selling, on the other hand, involves suggesting complementary products or services that enhance the customer's experience or address related needs.

Upselling Techniques

The first upselling technique is highlighting value-added features. When upselling, emphasize the additional features, benefits, or performance improvements that come with the higher-priced option. Explain how these enhancements can provide a superior experience or long-term cost savings. An example of this is,

> *HeatWave HVAC Solutions, who effectively upsold customers on high-efficiency HVAC systems by highlighting their energy-saving features and the potential for reduced utility bills. They explained how the upfront investment would pay off over time and provided supporting statistics on energy savings.*

The second is offering extended warranties or service plans. Upselling extended warranties or service plans can provide customers with peace of mind and added value. Explain the benefits of extended coverage, such as priority service, discounted repairs, or extended lifespan of their HVAC system.

> *SwiftFix HVAC Services successfully upsold customers on extended service plans by emphasizing the value of comprehensive coverage and the potential savings on future repairs. They highlighted the convenience of priority service and the peace of mind it provides to customers.*

Cross-Selling Techniques

Be sure you are identifying complementary products or services. Analyze your product and service offerings to identify items that naturally complement each other. Recommend these complementary offerings to customers, explaining how they can enhance their HVAC system's performance or address related needs.

According to a study by Accenture, 91% of consumers are more likely to shop with brands that provide relevant offers and recommendations.

One such relevant offer would be to successfully cross-sell customers on programmable thermostats when installing new HVAC systems. You can explain how a programmable thermostat could optimize energy efficiency and improve comfort levels by automating temperature adjustments. This cross-selling strategy can enhance the customer's overall HVAC experience.

The next option is to bundle packages and promotions. Create bundled packages or promotional offers that combine multiple products or services at a discounted price. Highlight the cost-saving advantages of purchasing the bundle and explain how the bundled offerings work together to meet the customer's needs.

Reliable HVAC Contractors increased their revenue through cross-selling by offering bundled maintenance packages. They combined annual tune-ups, air filter replacements, and discounted repairs into a comprehensive package.

This provided customers with convenient, all-in-one maintenance solutions while increasing the average transaction value.

Effective Upselling and Cross-Selling Strategies

To ensure successful upselling and cross-selling, it's important to implement effective strategies that align with customer needs and preferences. Consider the following techniques:

1. Customer Needs Assessment: Before suggesting additional products or services, conduct a thorough assessment of the customer's needs. Understanding their pain points and goals allows you to make targeted recommendations that resonate with

their specific requirements.

ImagineCool HVAC Services conducted a detailed needs assessment before recommending any upsells or cross-sells. By understanding a customer's desire for enhanced indoor air quality, they suggested a combination of an advanced filtration system and regular air quality testing.

This tailored solution addressed the customer's specific needs and exceeded their expectations.

2. Effective Communication and Education: Clearly communicate the benefits of the upsell or cross-sell offerings to customers. Explain how these additional products or services can enhance their HVAC system's performance, improve efficiency, or provide convenience and cost savings. According to a study by Statista, 73% of consumers are more likely to make a purchase if they have received proper education on the product or service.

AllSeasons HVAC Solutions excelled in upselling and cross-selling by effectively educating customers about the benefits of whole-house humidifiers. They explained how humidifiers could alleviate dry air symptoms, improve comfort, and even protect furniture and wooden structures.

This education-based approach increased customer awareness and resulted in successful upsells.

Upselling and cross-selling techniques are powerful strategies for increasing revenue and enhancing the customer experience in the HVAC industry. By implementing effective upselling and cross-selling techniques such as highlighting value-added features, offering extended warranties, identifying complementary products or services, and bundling packages, you can maximize the value of each customer interaction.

Remember, understanding customer needs, effectively communicating the benefits, and tailoring your recommendations are essential for successful upselling and cross-selling. By adopting these techniques and continuously refining your approach, you can drive revenue growth, exceed customer expectations, and build long-lasting relationships with your HVAC customers.

Before you move on....

1. Review your current lead generation strategies and identify one area where you can improve or expand your efforts. Develop a plan to implement this improvement within the next month and set measurable goals to track the success of your lead generation activities.

2. Enhance your customer relationship management (CRM) system or implement a new CRM tool to streamline your sales process and effectively track customer interactions. Train your team on how to use the CRM system to manage leads and nurture customer relationships.

3. Identify opportunities for upselling and cross-selling additional HVAC services to your existing customer base. Develop a strategy and sales script to introduce these services during customer interactions. Implement this upselling and cross-selling strategy with at least three existing customers within the next month.

PART 3

*Service Excellence and
Business Growth*

Welcome to Part 3 of our book, where we dive into the essential elements of service excellence and business growth in the HVAC industry. In this section, we will explore strategies and techniques to elevate your customer service, scale up your business, and develop your leadership skills. By focusing on delivering exceptional service experiences, expanding your offerings, and nurturing a thriving team, you can achieve long-term success in the HVAC business.

Chapter 7: Customer-Centric Service: Creating Wow Experiences

In Chapter 7, we will explore the power of customer-centric service and how it can set you apart from your competitors. We'll discuss the importance of delivering exceptional service at every touchpoint, from the initial customer contact to post-service follow-ups. We'll delve into effective communication techniques, active listening skills, and strategies for managing customer expectations and handling complaints. Get ready to wow your customers and build strong relationships that drive loyalty and referrals.

Chapter 8: Scaling Up: Growing Your HVAC Business for Long-Term Success

In Chapter 8, we shift our focus to business growth and scaling up your HVAC operations. We'll explore strategies for expanding your service offerings to meet the evolving needs of your customers. We'll also delve into building strategic partnerships and alliances that can fuel your growth and open new avenues for success. We'll guide you on managing growth while maintaining quality, ensuring that your business thrives as it expands.

Chapter 9: From Technician to Leader: Developing Your Leadership Skills

Chapter 9 is dedicated to helping you make the transition from a technical role to a managerial position. We'll explore the critical aspects of leadership development in the HVAC industry. You'll learn how to build a strong company culture, foster team morale, and effectively delegate tasks to empower your team. Developing your leadership skills is key to creating a high-performing team and achieving your business goals.

Conclusion: Achieving HVAC Business Mastery

In the conclusion, we will recap the key takeaways from each part of the book, highlighting the critical strategies and insights you have gained. We'll emphasize the importance of implementing the knowledge and techniques shared throughout the book to achieve HVAC business mastery. You'll be equipped with the tools and mindset to navigate the ever-changing landscape of the industry and drive your business to new heights.

CHAPTER 7

*Customer-Centric Service:
Creating Wow Experiences*

Delivering exceptional customer service is the key to creating lasting impressions, building strong relationships, and standing out from your competitors. A customer-centric approach goes beyond merely meeting expectations; it's about going above and beyond to create wow experiences that leave a lasting positive impact. In this chapter, we will explore strategies, stories, anecdotes, examples, and statistics to help you provide customer-centric service at every touchpoint. Get ready to elevate your customer interactions and create wow experiences that will make your HVAC business shine.

Delivering Exceptional Service at Every Touchpoint

To create wow experiences, it's crucial to provide exceptional service at every customer touchpoint. From the first phone call to post-service follow-ups, each interaction is an opportunity to exceed expectations and leave a lasting impression. Consider the following strategies:

1. Warm and Friendly Greetings: Start every interaction with a warm and friendly greeting. Whether it's answering the phone or greeting customers at their doorstep, a genuine smile and a positive attitude can set the tone for a memorable experience.

SunHeat HVAC mastered the art of warm greetings by

training their team to answer calls with enthusiasm and genuine care. By making customers feel valued and appreciated from the very beginning, they set the stage for an exceptional service experience.

2. Prompt and Effective Communication: Effective communication is crucial in providing exceptional service. Respond promptly to customer inquiries, listen actively to their needs, and communicate clearly throughout the service process. Be proactive in providing updates or addressing any concerns that arise.

SwiftCool HVAC Services prided themselves on their prompt and effective communication. They implemented a system that ensured customers were informed about service appointments, including details such as technician arrival times. This proactive communication helped build trust and enhanced the overall service experience.

Active Listening and Understanding Customer Needs

Active listening is a powerful tool in providing customer-centric service. By truly understanding your customers' needs, you can tailor your solutions to meet their specific requirements. Consider the following strategies:

1. Asking Open-Ended Questions: Encourage customers to share their concerns and goals by asking open-ended questions. This allows them to express themselves fully and provides valuable insights for delivering personalized solutions.

ComfortZone HVAC Solutions engaged in active listening by asking open-ended questions such as, "Tell me about the issues you're experiencing with your HVAC system." By encouraging customers to share their experiences, they gained a deeper understanding of their needs and could offer tailored solutions.

2. Empathizing and Providing Solutions: Show empathy and understanding towards customers' challenges and frustrations. Put yourself in their shoes, acknowledge their concerns, and provide solutions that address their specific issues.

Reliable Air Solutions trained their technicians to empathize with customers who were facing HVAC system breakdowns during extreme weather conditions. They understood the stress and discomfort it caused and went the extra mile to expedite the repairs. This empathetic approach not only solved the immediate issue but also built customer loyalty and trust.

Managing Customer Expectations and Handling Complaints

Proactively managing customer expectations and effectively handling complaints are crucial aspects of providing exceptional service. Addressing concerns promptly and effectively can turn a negative experience into a positive one. Consider the following strategies:

Set clear expectations about the scope of your services, estimated timelines, and any potential disruptions. Be transparent about what customers can expect throughout the service process, ensuring there are no surprises along the way.

ImagineComfort HVAC Services took proactive measures to manage customer expectations. They provided detailed explanations about the service process, including the steps involved and any potential inconveniences. This transparency fostered trust and reduced customer anxieties.

When complaints arise, view them as opportunities to turn dissatisfied customers into loyal advocates. Actively listen to their concerns, apologize sincerely, and provide a fair and timely resolution. Going the extra mile to rectify issues demonstrates your commitment to customer satisfaction.

Providing customer-centric service is the cornerstone of success in the HVAC industry. By delivering exceptional service at every touchpoint, actively listening to customer needs, managing expectations, and handling complaints effectively, you can create wow experiences that set your HVAC business apart.

Through the strategies, stories, anecdotes, examples, and statistics shared in this chapter, you have gained actionable insights to elevate your customer interactions and provide exceptional service. Remember, it's the small details and personal touches that make a difference in creating memorable experiences. By consistently exceeding customer expectations, you will build strong relationships, foster customer loyalty, and fuel the growth of your HVAC business.

Creating Exceptional Service and Wow Experiences

In the HVAC industry, providing exceptional service and creating wow experiences is crucial for building strong customer relationships and standing out in a competitive market. Exceptional service goes beyond meeting basic expectations; it's about exceeding customer expectations and leaving a lasting positive impression. In this chapter, we will explore strategies, statistics, case studies, and examples to help you create exceptional service and wow experiences for your customers. Get ready to elevate your service game and leave a lasting impact on every customer.

Understanding the Power of Exceptional Service

Exceptional service has a profound impact on customer satisfaction, loyalty, and word-of-mouth referrals. By going above and beyond, you can create memorable experiences that customers will rave about. Consider the following strategies:

Be sure to anticipate customer needs. Proactively anticipate customer needs by understanding their pain points and preferences. According to a study by PwC, 59% of consumers would try a new brand or company for a better service experience. So, be prepared to provide solutions or recommendations before they even ask, showing your attentiveness and commitment to their satisfaction.

SwiftHeat HVAC Services excelled in anticipating customer needs. When performing routine maintenance, their technicians inspected the entire HVAC system and identified potential issues before they became major problems. By addressing these concerns proactively, they delighted customers and prevented costly breakdowns.

Be sure to personalize the service experience. Tailor your service to each customer's unique preferences and requirements. Show genuine interest in their specific needs, and customize your approach accordingly.

Creating Wow Experiences

Wow experiences are the moments that truly leave a lasting impact on customers. They go beyond what is expected, surprising and delighting customers in unexpected ways. This can be done by, going the extra mile. Look for opportunities to go above and beyond to create memorable experiences. Whether it's providing a small complimentary service or offering unexpected perks, these gestures can make a big difference.

Much like in this example where, ComfortCare HVAC Services

went the extra mile by providing complimentary air quality testing with their regular maintenance service. This additional value-added service surprised customers and showcased the company's commitment to their well-being.

Go beyond with personalized surprises, surprise customers with personalized touches that show you've gone the extra mile to make their experience special. This could be anything from a handwritten thank-you note to a small gift related to their HVAC system.

AirComfort HVAC Solutions delighted their customers by sending personalized thank-you notes after each service appointment. The notes expressed gratitude for their business and included a small magnet with helpful tips for maintaining optimal HVAC system performance. These personalized surprises left a lasting positive impression.

Building a Customer-Centric Culture

To consistently deliver exceptional service and wow experiences, it's important to foster a customer-centric culture within your HVAC business.

This starts with training and empowering your employees. Provide comprehensive training to your employees on customer service skills, empathy, and problem-solving. Empower them to make decisions that prioritize the customer's best interests.

When you invest in extensive training programs for your employees or technicians, focusing not only on technical skills but also on customer service excellence. This will empower your technicians to make on-the-spot decisions that prioritized customer satisfaction, leading to positive experiences for your customers.

Seek continuous improvement and feedback from your

customers. Regularly seek feedback from customers to identify areas for improvement. Use this feedback to refine your processes, address any gaps in service, and continually enhance the customer experience.

ClimateControl HVAC Services implemented a customer feedback system that allowed customers to rate their service experience and provide comments. They used this feedback to identify patterns, address any issues, and recognize employees who consistently delivered exceptional service.

Creating exceptional service and wow experiences is a powerful way to differentiate your HVAC business and build lasting customer relationships. By anticipating customer needs, personalizing the service experience, going the extra mile, and fostering a customer-centric culture, you can elevate your service game and leave a lasting positive impression.

Through the strategies, statistics, case studies, and examples shared in this chapter, you have gained actionable insights to create exceptional service and wow experiences. Remember, it's the little details, personalized touches, and genuine care that make a significant impact on customer satisfaction and loyalty. By consistently delivering exceptional service, you can set your HVAC business apart and become a customer favorite in your market.

Fostering a Customer-Centric Culture and Handling Negative Feedback

Fostering a customer-centric culture is essential for creating exceptional service experiences and building strong customer relationships in the HVAC industry. A customer-centric culture puts the customer at the heart of your business, guiding decision-making, behaviors, and interactions.

Creating a Customer-Centric Culture

Building a customer-centric culture starts from within your organization. It involves instilling a mindset that prioritizes customer satisfaction and aligning every aspect of your business towards this goal. We do that with two main ideas:

1. Clearly Define and Communicate Customer-Centric Values: Start by clearly defining the values that reflect a customer-centric culture. Communicate these values to all employees and reinforce them regularly. Emphasize the importance of putting the customer first in every interaction. This is important because according to a study by Deloitte, customer-centric companies are 60% more profitable compared to companies that are not focused on the customer.

ComfortCare HVAC Services developed a set of customer-centric values that guided their employees' behavior. These values, including empathy, integrity, and responsiveness, were communicated through regular team meetings, training sessions, and displayed prominently in the workplace. This clarity helped create a unified and customer-focused team.

2. Empower and Train Employees: Empower your employees to make decisions and take actions that prioritize customer satisfaction. Provide comprehensive training on customer service skills, problem-solving, and conflict resolution. Equip them with the tools and knowledge needed to excel in customer interactions.

Handling Negative Feedback

Negative feedback is an opportunity for growth and improvement. By handling negative feedback effectively, you can turn a dissatisfied customer into a loyal advocate.

1. Actively Listen and Acknowledge the Feedback: When receiving negative feedback, approach it with an open mind and a willingness to understand the customer's perspective. Actively listen to their concerns and acknowledge their feelings, demonstrating empathy and a genuine desire to address the issue.

AirTech HVAC Solutions made it a priority to actively listen and acknowledge negative feedback. When a customer expressed dissatisfaction with a service, they took the time to understand the issue, apologized sincerely, and assured the customer that they would resolve the problem promptly. This empathetic approach diffused the situation and allowed them to turn the negative experience into a positive one.

2. Take Immediate Action and Find Solutions: Once you understand the customer's concerns, take immediate action to resolve the issue. Communicate transparently with the customer, provide regular updates on the progress, and ensure a satisfactory resolution is achieved.

Reliable Air Solutions implemented a structured process for handling negative feedback. They assigned a dedicated customer service representative to handle complaints, ensuring that each issue was addressed promptly and effectively. They made it a priority to communicate with customers throughout the resolution process, ensuring transparency and trust.

3. Learn and Improve: Treat negative feedback as an opportunity for learning and improvement. Analyze the feedback to identify patterns or areas where your business can enhance its service. Use

the insights gained to refine your processes, provide additional training to employees, and implement changes that prevent similar issues from recurring.

> *Sunshine HVAC Services conducted regular internal reviews to analyze negative feedback and identify areas for improvement. They used this feedback to refine their service delivery processes, address training gaps, and implement quality control measures. This continuous improvement approach helped them consistently deliver exceptional service.*

Fostering a customer-centric culture and effectively handling negative feedback are vital for creating exceptional service experiences and building strong customer relationships in the HVAC industry. By clearly defining customer-centric values, empowering and training employees, actively listening to feedback, taking immediate action to resolve issues, and using feedback as a tool for learning and improvement, you can create a culture that consistently delivers exceptional service and turns negative experiences into positive ones.

Through the strategies, statistics, case studies, and examples shared in this chapter, you have gained actionable insights to foster a customer-centric culture and handle negative feedback effectively. Remember, a customer-centric culture starts from within and requires a commitment from every member of your team. By prioritizing the customer and using negative feedback as an opportunity for growth, you can build a reputation for exceptional service and cultivate long-lasting customer loyalty.

Before you move on....

1. Conduct a customer satisfaction survey or feedback campaign to gauge your customers' experiences and identify areas for improvement. Use the feedback received to develop

an action plan to address any recurring issues or concerns. Implement at least one improvement initiative within the next two months.

2. Train your team on effective communication techniques and active listening skills. Conduct role-playing exercises to practice empathetic listening and responding to customer inquiries or concerns. Schedule regular team meetings to discuss customer communication strategies and share best practices.

3. Create a system for managing and resolving customer complaints effectively. Establish clear protocols for acknowledging and addressing complaints promptly and professionally. Develop a step-by-step guide for your team to follow when handling customer complaints and make it easily accessible to all team members.

CHAPTER 8

Scaling Up: Growing Your HVAC Business for Long-Term Success

Scaling up your operations is a crucial step towards long-term success. Scaling up involves expanding your service offerings, building strategic partnerships, and managing growth while maintaining quality. In this chapter, we will explore practical strategies, anecdotes, examples, and statistics to help you navigate the challenges and seize the opportunities that come with scaling up your HVAC business. Get ready to unlock your business's growth potential and achieve sustainable success.

Expanding Your Service Offerings

Expanding your service offerings is a key component of scaling up your HVAC business. By diversifying your services, you can attract a broader customer base, increase revenue streams, and position your business as a one-stop solution provider.

Stay ahead of the curve by identifying emerging trends and market gaps in the HVAC industry. Monitor industry developments, customer demands, and technological advancements to identify new service opportunities. According to a report by Grand View Research, the global HVAC systems market size is projected to reach $241.8 billion by 2028.

Next, offer maintenance plans and service contracts. Develop comprehensive maintenance plans and service contracts to provide ongoing support and value to your customers. These plans can include regular inspections, preventative maintenance, priority service, and discounts on repairs.

Building Strategic Partnerships and Alliances

Strategic partnerships and alliances can be instrumental in scaling up your HVAC business. By collaborating with complementary businesses, you can expand your reach, access new markets, and leverage each other's strengths.

1. Partnering with Contractors in Related Industries: Identify contractors in related industries, such as plumbing or electrical, and establish strategic partnerships. Collaborate on joint marketing efforts, referral programs, and cross-promotion to tap into each other's customer bases.

2. Collaborating with Manufacturers and Suppliers: Forge strong relationships with manufacturers and suppliers in the HVAC industry. By establishing partnerships, you can gain access to exclusive products, negotiate favorable pricing, and stay updated on industry advancements.

Managing Growth While Maintaining Quality

As your HVAC business scales up, it's essential to maintain high-quality service delivery. Consistency and reliability are key to preserving customer satisfaction and ensuring continued success. In order to sustain these we need to implement two things, Processes/quality control and training/development. With these in mind as we scale up, we will be able to maintain the high level of service we currently offer.

1. Streamline Processes and Implement Quality Control Measures: As your business grows, streamline your internal processes to ensure efficiency and consistency. Implement quality control measures to maintain service standards and ensure that every customer receives the same level of excellence.

2. Invest in Training and Development: As your team grows, invest in training and development programs to ensure that employees have the skills and knowledge to deliver exceptional service. Provide ongoing learning opportunities and empower employees to take ownership of their professional growth.

> *EliteAir HVAC Services established a comprehensive training program that included technical training, customer service skills development, and leadership workshops. They believed that investing in their employees' growth would result in a highly skilled and motivated team that could meet the demands of their growing customer base.*

Scaling up your HVAC business is a thrilling journey that requires careful planning, strategic decision-making, and a customer-centric approach. By expanding your service offerings, building strategic partnerships, and maintaining high-quality service delivery, you can achieve sustainable growth and long-term success.

Scaling up is not just about expansion; it's about ensuring that your business maintains its reputation for excellence and customer satisfaction as it grows. Embrace the opportunities that come with scaling up, adapt to market changes, and continue delivering exceptional service to drive your HVAC business towards new heights of success.

Expanding Your Service Offerings

Expanding your service offerings is a strategic move that can propel your HVAC business to new heights. By diversifying the services you provide, you can attract a broader customer base, increase revenue streams, and position your business as a comprehensive solution provider. In this chapter, we will explore practical strategies, statistics, case studies, and examples to guide you in expanding your service offerings and unlocking new growth opportunities. Get ready to embrace innovation, meet evolving customer demands, and take your HVAC business to the next level.

Identifying Emerging Trends and Market Gaps

To effectively expand your service offerings, it's essential to stay ahead of emerging trends and identify market gaps in the HVAC industry. By monitoring industry developments, customer demands, and technological advancements, you can identify new service opportunities.

Stay Informed about Technological Advancements: Keep abreast of the latest technological advancements in the HVAC industry. Innovations such as smart home automation, energy-efficient systems, and indoor air quality solutions present new avenues for service expansion. Listen to customer feedback and needs. Always pay close attention to customer feedback and identify any recurring requests or pain points. This valuable insight can guide you in expanding your services to address customer needs more comprehensively.

ComfortZone HVAC Services actively sought feedback from their customers and noticed a common desire for more comprehensive indoor air quality solutions. They responded by expanding their service offerings to include air purification systems, humidity control solutions, and duct cleaning services. This proactive approach not only met customer demands but also increased customer satisfaction and loyalty.

Offering Maintenance Plans and Service Contracts

Developing comprehensive maintenance plans and service contracts is an effective way to expand your service offerings while providing ongoing support to your customers. These plans can include regular inspections, preventative maintenance, priority service, and discounts on repairs.

Tailor maintenance plans to customer needs. Customize your maintenance plans to address the specific needs of your customers. Offer different tiers of plans that cater to various budgets and service requirements, providing flexibility and value to customers.

ReliableAir HVAC Services introduced a range of maintenance plans tailored to their customers' needs. They offered basic plans for routine inspections and filter changes, as well as comprehensive plans that included additional services like coil cleaning and priority scheduling. These plans provided peace of mind to customers and generated recurring revenue for the business.

Be sure to highlight the benefits of service contracts. Clearly communicate the benefits of service contracts to your customers. Emphasize how contracts can help prevent costly breakdowns, extend the lifespan of their HVAC systems, and provide priority service during peak seasons.

ProActive HVAC Solutions educated their customers about the advantages of service contracts through informative brochures and website content. They emphasized that contracts not only save money in the long run but also ensure that customers receive prompt and reliable service when they need it most.

Expanding your service offerings is a strategic step towards growth and success in the HVAC industry. By identifying emerging trends, addressing market gaps, and diversifying your services, you can attract a wider customer base and increase revenue streams.

Expanding your service offerings requires a customer-centric approach, innovation, and a commitment to delivering exceptional service. Continually monitor industry trends, listen to customer feedback, and adapt your offerings to meet evolving demands. By expanding your service offerings, you can position your HVAC business as a comprehensive solution provider and cement your reputation as a leader in the industry.

Building Strategic Partnerships and Alliances

Building strategic partnerships and alliances is a powerful strategy for scaling up your HVAC business and unlocking new growth opportunities. By collaborating with complementary businesses, you can expand your reach, access new markets, and leverage each other's strengths. Get ready to forge valuable connections, enhance your competitive advantage, and take your HVAC business to new heights.

Partnering with Contractors in Related Industries

One effective way to build strategic partnerships is by collaborating with contractors in related industries. By forming alliances with businesses such as plumbing or electrical contractors, you can create mutually beneficial relationships that open doors to new customers and synergistic opportunities.

Start by identifying complementary contractors. Seek out contractors in related industries that offer services that complement your HVAC business. Look for businesses that share similar customer profiles or work in the same geographic area to maximize the synergy of your partnership.

Integrated Solutions HVAC and Plumbing recognized the opportunity to offer comprehensive home services to their customers. By forming a strategic partnership, they were able to refer customers in need of HVAC or plumbing services, providing a seamless experience and expanding their service capabilities. This partnership resulted in increased customer satisfaction and revenue growth for both companies.

Search for companies to collaborate on joint marketing efforts. Join forces with your partner businesses to implement joint marketing initiatives. By pooling resources and sharing marketing costs, you can reach a larger audience and amplify the impact of your marketing campaigns.

ClimateControl HVAC and Electrical Services formed a collaborative marketing campaign with an electrical contractor. They jointly sponsored local community events, created co-branded marketing materials, and shared social media promotions. This partnership increased brand visibility and attracted customers seeking both HVAC and electrical services.

Collaborating with Manufacturers and Suppliers

Forming strong relationships with manufacturers and suppliers in the HVAC industry can bring numerous benefits to your business. According to a survey by Deloitte, 47% of businesses reported that their strategic partnerships improved their ability to develop innovative products and services. These partnerships can give you access to exclusive products, provide insights on industry trends, and offer competitive advantages. Consider the following,

1. Establish Mutually Beneficial Partnerships: Identify reputable manufacturers and suppliers in the HVAC industry that align with your business values and goals. Seek out companies that offer high-quality products, reliable support, and competitive pricing.

2. Stay Informed about Industry Developments: Maintain regular communication with your manufacturing and supply partners to stay informed about industry developments. Attend industry conferences, participate in training programs, and engage in discussions to gain insights on emerging technologies, product advancements, and market trends.

Building strategic partnerships and alliances is a powerful strategy for expanding your HVAC business and enhancing your competitive advantage. By collaborating with complementary contractors in related industries and forming partnerships with manufacturers and suppliers, you can access new markets, increase your service capabilities, and leverage each other's strengths.

Nurture your relationships, seek out synergistic opportunities, and continue to adapt and evolve your partnerships as your business grows. By building strategic partnerships and alliances, you can unlock new growth opportunities and establish your HVAC business as a trusted industry leader.

Managing Growth While Maintaining Quality

As your HVAC business scales up and experiences growth, it's essential to maintain high-quality service delivery. Consistency and reliability are key to preserving customer satisfaction and ensuring continued success. Get ready to navigate the challenges of expansion, preserve your reputation for excellence, and drive sustainable success.

Streamlining Processes and Implementing Quality Control Measures

Maintaining quality while managing growth requires streamlining processes and implementing effective quality control measures. By optimizing your operations, you can ensure consistency, efficiency, and customer satisfaction.

Regularly assess your internal processes to identify bottlenecks, inefficiencies, and areas for improvement. Streamline workflows, eliminate unnecessary steps, and leverage technology to enhance operational efficiency.

Establish quality control measures to ensure that consistent and high-quality service is delivered to your customers. Develop standards, checklists, and protocols that guide your team in delivering exceptional service and meeting customer expectations.

ReliableHeat HVAC Solutions implemented a quality control program that included regular inspections, performance tracking, and customer feedback analysis. This allowed them to identify areas for improvement, address any service gaps, and ensure that their technicians consistently delivered high-quality workmanship.

Investing in Training and Development

As your team grows, investing in training and development becomes crucial for maintaining quality. By providing ongoing learning opportunities, you can equip your employees with the necessary skills, knowledge, and confidence to deliver exceptional service.

Provide comprehensive onboarding and training. Develop a comprehensive onboarding program to ensure that new hires are aligned with your quality standards and service expectations. Provide initial training on technical skills, customer service, and company culture to set a strong foundation for delivering exceptional service.

Provide ongoing professional development! Foster a culture of continuous learning and development within your HVAC business. Provide opportunities for your team to attend workshops, conferences, and industry events. Encourage them to pursue certifications and participate in online training programs to enhance their skills and stay updated on industry best practices.

SkilledAir HVAC Solutions supported their technicians' professional development by providing access to industry training programs and certifications. By investing in their employees' growth, they not only improved the technical proficiency of their team but also increased customer confidence in their ability to deliver high-quality service.

Managing growth while maintaining quality is a balancing act that requires attention to detail, streamlined processes, and a commitment to ongoing improvement. By streamlining your operations, implementing quality control measures, investing in training and development, and fostering a culture of continuous improvement, you can successfully navigate the challenges of expansion while delivering exceptional service to your customers.

Maintaining quality is the foundation of your business's reputation and long-term success. By prioritizing quality at every stage of growth, you can preserve customer satisfaction, build a loyal customer base, and establish your HVAC business as a trusted industry leader.

Before you move on....

1. Research and evaluate potential expansion opportunities within the HVAC industry, such as offering specialized services or entering new geographic markets. Identify the most viable opportunity for your business and develop a detailed growth plan, including timelines, resource requirements, and potential risks.

2. Explore strategic partnerships or alliances with complementary businesses, such as plumbers or electricians, to expand your service offerings or reach new customers. Reach out to potential partners and initiate discussions to explore collaboration opportunities.

3. Develop a system for measuring and monitoring key performance indicators (KPIs) to track the growth and success of your HVAC business. Identify the relevant KPIs for your business, such as revenue growth, customer retention rate, or average job size. Implement a tracking system and regularly review and analyze your KPIs to make data-driven decisions for future growth.

CHAPTER 9

From Technician to Leader:
Developing Your Leadership Skills

Transitioning from a technical role to a leadership position is a critical step in driving your business towards long-term success. Developing strong leadership skills is essential for effectively managing your team, fostering a positive company culture, and driving growth. In this chapter, we will explore practical strategies, stories, anecdotes, examples, and statistics to help you develop your leadership skills and thrive as a leader in the HVAC industry. Get ready to unlock your leadership potential, inspire your team, and achieve remarkable results.

Transitioning from Technical Expert to Leader

Moving from a technical expert to a leader requires a shift in mindset and the development of new skills. It's important to balance your technical expertise with the ability to lead and inspire your team. Recognize that leadership is an ongoing journey of growth and development. Seek out learning opportunities, attend leadership workshops, read books on leadership, and learn from the experiences of other successful leaders.

Transitioning from a technical role to a leadership position requires a shift in mindset. Recognize that your role is not only about technical proficiency but also about guiding and supporting your team towards achieving common goals.

Sarah, a skilled technician at CoolBreeze HVAC Services, was promoted to a managerial role. She initially struggled with the transition, as she was accustomed to focusing solely on technical tasks. However, with guidance and mentorship, Sarah shifted her mindset, embraced her new responsibilities, and began to see herself as a leader. This change in mindset allowed her to effectively manage her team and drive their success.

Building a Strong Company Culture

A strong company culture is essential for creating a positive work environment and motivating your team. As a leader, you have the power to shape the culture of your HVAC business. You do this by following two simple steps.

1. Define Your Core Values: Clearly define the core values that will guide your business and reflect the culture you want to foster. Communicate these values to your team and lead by example in embodying them.

2. Encourage Open Communication: Foster a culture of open communication where every team member feels heard and valued. Encourage feedback, provide opportunities for collaboration, and create a safe space for sharing ideas and concerns.

OpenDoor HVAC Solutions implemented an open-door policy, where employees were encouraged to approach leaders with their thoughts, suggestions, and challenges. Regular team meetings and feedback sessions were held to promote open dialogue and ensure that everyone had a voice. This culture of open communication led to increased employee engagement and a sense of ownership among the team.

Effective Delegation and Talent Development

Delegating tasks and developing the talents of your team members are crucial aspects of leadership. Effective delegation allows you to focus on strategic initiatives while empowering your team to take ownership of their work. Get to know your team members' strengths, skills, and interests. Assign tasks and responsibilities that align with their capabilities, allowing them to excel and grow in their respective areas.

Support the growth and development of your team members by providing training opportunities, mentorship programs, and career advancement pathways. Encourage them to expand their skills, pursue certifications, and take on new challenges.

Developing your leadership skills is a transformative journey that requires continuous learning, a shift in mindset, and a commitment to fostering a positive company culture. By transitioning from a technical expert to a leader, building a strong company culture, and effectively delegating tasks while developing the talents of your team, you can become a successful leader in the HVAC industry.

Embrace the challenges and opportunities that come with leadership, inspire your team, and lead your HVAC business towards remarkable success. Leadership is not just about achieving individual goals; it's about empowering others to reach their full potential and driving the collective success of your organization.

Building a Strong Company Culture and Team Morale

Building a strong company culture and fostering high team

morale are essential for the success and growth of your HVAC business. A positive work environment not only attracts top talent but also motivates and engages your team, resulting in increased productivity and customer satisfaction. Get ready to create an environment where your team thrives, collaboration flourishes, and your HVAC business excels.

Defining Your Company Values

Defining and embodying your company values is the foundation of a strong company culture. When values are clear and consistently demonstrated, they shape behaviors, decisions, and interactions within your organization. Which is why we always want to identify our core values as an organization and then lead by example.

We identify the core values that align with your HVAC business's mission, vision, and desired culture. These values should guide your actions, define expectations, and serve as a compass for decision-making.

Once we have identified and established our values we then have to lead by example. As a leader, it's essential to embody the values you expect from your team. Demonstrate behaviors that reflect your company values in your interactions with employees, customers, and partners. This sets the tone and reinforces the importance of the values in your organization.

Nurturing Collaboration and Team Spirit

Collaboration and a sense of camaraderie among team members are vital for building a strong company culture and boosting team morale. When employees feel connected and supported, they are more engaged and motivated. Create a culture of open communication where employees feel comfortable sharing ideas, providing feedback, and expressing their concerns. Encourage regular team meetings, brainstorming sessions, and opportunities for cross-departmental collaboration.

At DynamicAir HVAC Solutions, regular team meetings were held to encourage collaboration and idea sharing. During one of these meetings, a technician shared a creative solution to a recurring problem. The idea was implemented, resulting in improved efficiency and customer satisfaction. This collaborative environment not only empowered team members but also fostered a sense of ownership and pride in their work.

Encourage teamwork and support among employees by recognizing and appreciating their contributions. Create opportunities for team-building activities, such as group projects, team outings, or volunteer initiatives, that strengthen bonds and foster a positive work culture.

Recognizing and Rewarding Achievements

Recognizing and rewarding employee achievements is a powerful way to boost team morale and reinforce desired behaviors within your organization. It fosters a culture of appreciation and motivates employees to perform at their best. Recognize individual and team achievements, such as meeting targets, completing challenging projects, or going above and beyond to deliver exceptional service. Celebrate these milestones publicly and acknowledge the efforts that led to their success.

Provide growth and development opportunities. Support employee growth and development by offering training programs, mentorship opportunities, and career advancement pathways. When employees see opportunities for personal and professional growth within your organization, their morale and loyalty increase.

Building a strong company culture and fostering high team morale are essential for the long-term success of your

HVAC business. By defining your company values, nurturing collaboration and team spirit, and recognizing and rewarding achievements, you can create an environment where your team thrives and your business excels.

A strong company culture is built over time and requires consistent effort. Lead by example, encourage collaboration, and create a supportive environment that motivates and empowers your team. When you prioritize your team's well-being and foster a sense of belonging, your HVAC business will flourish.

Effective Delegation and Talent Development

Effective delegation and talent development are crucial aspects of leadership that contribute to the growth and success of your HVAC business. Delegating tasks and developing the talents of your team members not only empowers them but also allows you to focus on strategic initiatives and drive overall productivity. Get ready to maximize the potential of your team and achieve remarkable results.

Identifying Strengths and Assigning Responsibilities

Understanding the strengths and capabilities of your team members is the key to effective delegation. By assigning tasks and responsibilities that align with their strengths, you can optimize productivity and foster individual growth. Consider the following strategies:

Take the time to assess and understand the unique strengths and skills of each team member. Observe their performance, solicit their input, and conduct conversations to identify their areas of expertise. Once you have identified individual strengths, delegate tasks and responsibilities that allow team members to leverage their expertise. Provide clear instructions, set realistic expectations, and empower them to take ownership of their work.

Investing in Talent Development

Fostering the growth and development of your team members is essential for their long-term success and the overall success of your HVAC business. According to LinkedIn's Workplace Learning Report, 94% of employees would stay longer at a company if it invested in their career development. By providing training opportunities, mentorship, and career development pathways, you can unlock their potential and cultivate a culture of continuous improvement.

Make sure you provide relevant training opportunities. Offer relevant training programs, workshops, and seminars to enhance the skills and knowledge of your team members. Invest in industry certifications and encourage participation in professional development courses.

> *ProTech HVAC Services created a comprehensive training program that encompassed technical skills, customer service, and leadership development. They collaborated with industry experts to provide customized training sessions and encouraged employees to pursue industry certifications. This investment in training not only improved the skills of their team members but also boosted employee morale and retention.*

Establish a mentorship program where experienced team members can provide guidance, support, and professional advice to less experienced colleagues. Create opportunities for career advancement and growth by identifying potential leaders and offering them additional responsibilities.

> *Lisa, a technician at ReliableAir HVAC Solutions, expressed her interest in advancing her career within the company.*

The leadership recognized her potential and assigned her a mentor who provided guidance and support in developing her leadership skills. As a result, Lisa grew both professionally and personally, eventually transitioning into a supervisory role. This mentorship program not only empowered Lisa but also strengthened the talent pipeline within the organization.

Effective delegation and talent development are essential for maximizing the potential of your team and driving the success of your HVAC business. By identifying individual strengths and assigning responsibilities accordingly, you empower your team members to excel in their areas of expertise. Additionally, by investing in their growth and development through training opportunities and mentorship programs, you foster a culture of continuous improvement.

Effective delegation requires trust, clear communication, and providing support when needed. Likewise, talent development requires a commitment to providing learning opportunities and fostering a culture of mentorship and growth. By embracing these practices, you will not only optimize productivity and performance but also create a supportive and dynamic work environment where your team members can thrive.

Before you move on....

1. Assess your current leadership strengths and areas for improvement. Identify one specific leadership skill that you would like to develop further, such as effective delegation or conflict resolution. Seek out resources, such as books, courses, or workshops, to enhance your knowledge and practice this skill.

2. Foster a strong company culture by defining your core values and communicating them to your team. Develop initiatives or activities that promote teamwork, collaboration, and

employee engagement. Implement one new culture-building activity within the next quarter.

3. Invest in talent development by creating a training and development program for your team. Identify specific skills or areas of expertise that are essential for your business's success and design training modules or workshops to enhance those skills. Schedule regular training sessions and provide opportunities for your team members to grow and expand their capabilities.

CONCLUSION

Achieving HVAC Business Mastery

Congratulations on completing your journey towards achieving HVAC business mastery! Throughout this book, we have explored various aspects of building and growing a thriving HVAC business. From laying the foundation to winning in a competitive market, and from service excellence to business growth, you have gained valuable insights, strategies, and actionable advice to propel your business to new heights.

As you reflect on your journey, remember that success in the HVAC industry goes beyond technical expertise. It requires passion, an entrepreneurial mindset, and a commitment to continuous learning and growth. Let's recap some of the key takeaways from each part of this book:

Part 1: Laying the Foundation

In Part 1, we discussed the importance of discovering your passion for HVAC, developing an entrepreneurial mindset, and overcoming challenges. You have learned that success begins with aligning your work with your passion and embracing opportunities to innovate and adapt.

Part 2: Winning in a Competitive Market

Part 2 focused on branding and marketing mastery, pricing strategies, and sales excellence. You discovered the power of creating a compelling brand identity, designing effective marketing strategies, and leveraging digital channels for maximum impact. Additionally, you learned how to determine optimal pricing strategies, communicate value, and excel in consultative selling to convert leads into loyal customers.

Part 3: Service Excellence and Business Growth

In Part 3, we explored the importance of customer-centric service, scaling up your business, and developing your leadership skills. You discovered how delivering exceptional customer experiences, fostering a strong company culture, and effectively delegating tasks can contribute to long-term success. Furthermore, you learned how to expand your service offerings, build strategic partnerships, and develop the leadership skills necessary to drive growth.

As you implement the strategies and recommendations provided throughout this book, remember that your journey to HVAC business mastery is ongoing. The HVAC industry is dynamic, and staying ahead requires continuous learning, adaptation, and innovation. Embrace new technologies, stay informed about industry trends, and prioritize the development of your team and yourself.

As you embark on your journey towards HVAC business mastery, remember that it is not just about achieving individual goals. It is about creating a positive impact on your team, your customers, and the industry as a whole. Embrace the challenges, celebrate the successes, and always strive for excellence.

Use the resources, templates, and checklists provided in the appendix to support your continued growth and success. Additionally, stay connected with industry associations, attend conferences, and engage in networking opportunities to foster collaboration and stay abreast of industry advancements.

Thank you for joining us on this enlightening and empowering journey. By applying the knowledge, strategies, and actionable advice shared in this book, you are well-equipped to achieve HVAC business mastery. Remember, the sky is the limit, and your determination, combined with your newfound expertise, will lead you to remarkable success in the HVAC industry.

RESOURCES

Resources, Templates, and Checklists

Want to claim all the resources discussed in the book?

Head on over to <u>HVACBusinessGuide.com</u> to get the:

1. Business Plan Template

2. Marketing Strategy Template

3. Pricing Strategy Checklist

4. Customer Service Excellence Checklist

ABOUT THE AUTHOR

Epic Network

EPIC Network is a dynamic platform created with the mission to empower business owners, entrepreneurial investors, and service providers. Recognizing a significant gap in traditional business education, EPIC Network aims to revolutionize how individuals grow their wealth and impact the business world.

The network is committed to introducing a unique approach to Mergers & Acquisitions (M&A) - creative financing. Unlike conventional financing methods taught in most business programs, creative financing enables individuals and businesses to purchase businesses, traffic, and other wealth-creating assets without the need for out-of-pocket cash. EPIC Network not only introduces this innovative strategy but provides the requisite tools, trainings, and tactics to implement it successfully.

With a strong belief in the potential of every individual, EPIC Network offers its resources to both beginners and experts. The Network maintains that with commitment to success, there are no barriers that cannot be overcome.

At its core, EPIC Network is more than just an educational platform - it is a community that inspires, educates, and empowers individuals to grow their wealth and impact, thereby transforming the landscape of entrepreneurial finance and investment.